THE PRACTICAL
AUDIO-VISUAL
HANDBOOK
FOR TEACHERS

THE
PRACTICAL
AUDIO-

PARKER PUBLISHING COMPANY, INC.

West Nyack, New York

VISUAL
HANDBOOK
FOR TEACHERS

by

Herbert E.

Scuorzo, Ed.D.

THE PRACTICAL AUDIO-VISUAL HANDBOOK FOR TEACHERS

© 1967, BY

PARKER PUBLISHING COMPANY, INC.

WEST NYACK, N.Y.

LIBRARY OF CONGRESS
CATALOG CARD NUMBER: 67-16374

PRINTED IN THE UNITED STATES OF AMERICA
B & P

TO MY WIFE, LORETTA
and
TO LINDA, MARK,
AND KAREN

INTRODUCTION

Less than one teacher in four has taken a formal college course in audiovisual education. Few states require such training in teacher preparation. Startling? Yes—but lack of formal training does not show lack of teacher enthusiasm or interest.

In a recent survey by a leading national education magazine more teachers stated that they would like to see school funds spent on audiovisual materials than they would on salaries!

Obviously, then, school teachers understand the need for using AV methods in good teaching. Ideally, every school in the nation should have a "walking handbook"—an AV Building Coordinator, who can help teachers develop the AV presentations needed for optimum instruction. Unfortunately, this ideal is but a speck in the distant future—and teachers must teach *today's* children!

With but little formal audiovisual training, the teacher must develop for himself many of the most effective uses of materials and equipment. At best, this is a time consuming, if not impossible task. Unfortunately, for most already overburdened teachers, valuable audiovisual tools must remain unused. To fill this void, THE PRACTICAL AUDIOVISUAL HANDBOOK was developed.

The author, as a teacher himself, is well aware that this book—to be useful—must be designed for instant reference as a "desk" book, not a "library" book. It is an every-day book, not one for occasional reference.

Within these covers you will find "need-to-know" items about all audiovisual equipment and media needed by you—the classroom teacher.

There are extensive examples, hints, suggestions, and how-to-do-its for each AV medium, and indexing by subject area so that you can find "it" quickly.

This book is not a philosophical text on media and its effectiveness. It does not claim to be. It is a practical guide to the use of audiovisual materials in your classroom teaching.

Even with the plethora of ideas presented herein, you, as a good teacher, will continually think of new ways to adapt these ideas to your situation and class needs; or you'll develop wholly new ideas based on this book.

And in the long run, is this not the goal of both author and reader —to stimulate new ideas and use older ones effectively through audio-visual equipment and materials?

H. E. Scuorzo

Seton Hall University
South Orange, N.J.

CONTENTS

Chapter One

SLIDES
AND FILMSTRIPS

What visual aid do teachers use most? Probably the filmstrip/slide projector. So, if there's any way to begin a handbook, it's with the teacher's best friend!

Slides

Sizes. You can use a wide variety of slide sizes: 3¼ x 4 inch lantern slides, 2¼ x 2¼, 4 x 5, 2 x 2, and others. However, only two of them have real importance for school use—the 3¼ x 4 inch lantern slide and the 2 x 2 inch slide. The lantern slide is the older— and is considered by many to be the grandfather of visual education. The popularity of the lantern slide has declined since World War II, but the use of other sizes has skyrocketed. Still, you should be as familiar with the lantern slide as a basic teaching tool, as you are with the other slide sizes.

Lantern Slides. The lantern slide is usually made from a 3¼ x 4 inch piece of thin glass. Its working surface may be photographic emulsion, ground glass, gelatin coating, or clear glass. Lumarith® plastic, .02 inches thick, may be used in place of ground glass since both surfaces are matte and show a "tooth" to special slide crayons. The lantern slide must be sandwiched together with a clear glass slide (cover), and edge bound with binding tape.

A new type of lantern slide has been developed by the Polaroid Corporation. Like all Polaroid Land products, it features instantaneous development in the camera. This factor might bring about a re-birth of the lantern slide in American education.

2 x 2 Slides. This ubiquitous little item is a piece of 35 millimeter photographic film in a 2 by 2 inch cardboard, glass, or plastic mount.

1

Ordinarily, positive color film is used for 2 x 2 transparencies, but it is possible to make black-and-white slides if you need them for special purposes. For example, the copying of documents is best done on a special BW film called Micro-File® (Eastman Kodak Co.).

Unfortunately, a bit of semantic confusion exists with 2 x 2 slides. Some manufacturers refer to the picture size shown in Figure 1.1 as "half frame," while others call it "single frame." So too, with Figure 1.2. Some say "full frame," while others term it "double frame." The trend seems to be in favor of the terminology "half-frame" and "full frame," but by no means is the trend overwhelming!

Filmstrips

Filmstrips. The filmstrip (or slidefilm) is a series of half frame or full frame pictures on one strip of 35 mm film. Early filmstrips used the full frame format, but recent years find the half frame style becoming the standard for school use.

Slide and Filmstrip Projection. In all probability your school already has some kind of filmstrip or slide projection equipment. It may be a multiple use device, or it may project *only* slides, or *only* filmstrips. Multiple use machines generally have attachments to accomplish their purpose. And you need not operate the projector manually. In addition to manual machines, there are semi-automatic and automatic ones. While most *filmstrip* projectors or attachments require you to advance the film manually, the *slide* projector which only operates manually and with single slides is out-dated. With manual slide projection, you have the greatest possibility of error—improper slide insertion.

Semi-automatic and automatic slide projectors use trays or magazines for slide filing. Slides can't be improperly projected if they've been inserted into the holder correctly. The chief difference between the semi-automatic and the automatic slide projector is the manner in which slides are changed. The semi-automatic requires some action on the part of the operator, but the automatic can be set to operate itself and change slides at a predetermined interval.

In recent years, the increased popularity of dual slide presentations and multi-media demonstrations has led to the development of automatic dual projector systems which actually let you fade from one slide to another—or project both at once!

Using a Filmstrip Projector. The height of a teacher's embarrassing moments often occurs with the projection of a reversed or inverted

Fig. 1.1–2 by 2 inch half frame slide in cardboard mount.

Fig. 1.2–2 by 2 inch full frame slide in cardboard mount.

Fig. 1.3–Actual size filmstrip (35 mm wide). (*Society for Visual Education, Inc.*)

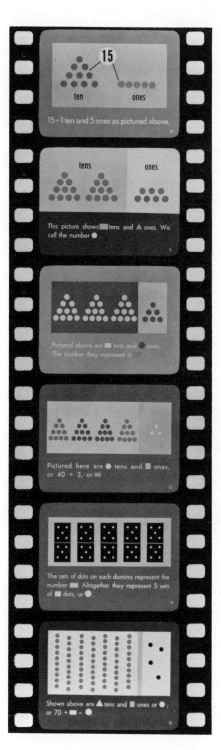

3

Fig. 1.4—The use of two projectors allows fading from one picture to another, or even superimposition or side by side projection. (*Eastman Kodak Company*)

Fig. 1.5a   Fig. 1.5b

An improperly framed filmstrip (left) can easily be corrected (right) by a simple adjustment of the framing control.

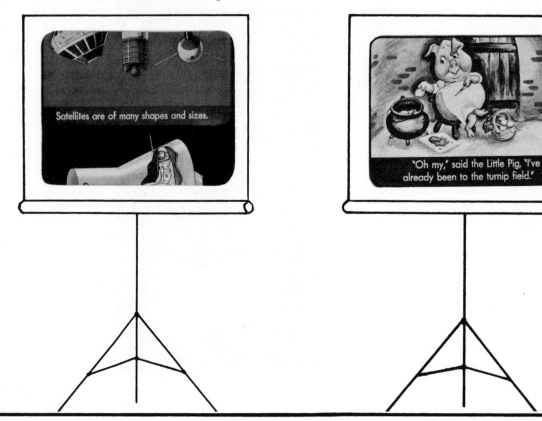

image. Pupils may find it amusing, but to most teachers, it is a bit disconcerting! A simple rule-of-thumb can prevent this error.

Most filmstrips have some method for indicating the beginning and end frames. The beginning may be a title frame; and the end may simply say "The End." With such a filmstrip, correct insertion is a simple matter. Using care not to touch the faces of the film, find the beginning of the filmstrip. Now, how do you insert it?

Point your projector toward the screen. Then stand behind the projector. Hold the filmstrip in such a manner that the title frame (beginning) reads from *right to left and upside-down* while you face the screen. Holding the filmstrip in exactly this position, insert it into the carrier of the projector. You'll always be correct!

If full frame filmstrips are used, insertion would be from the side of the projector—but the "upside down-right to left" rule still holds true.

Almost all filmstrip projectors have a framing control which allows you to place one whole picture on the screen, rather than two half pictures. Since it is next to impossible to insert the film in exactly the right frame position, the framing control is an essential tool.

Filmstrips depend, for their mechanical operation, on a harmonious marriage of sprocket holes on the filmstrip and sprocket teeth on the projector's film advance control. Projectors are pre-set so that operating the advance control moves the filmstrip exactly the right amount—thus assuring you that, once framed on the screen, your filmstrip will remain framed throughout its entire length. If proper framing is lost, it may mean that the film transport mechanism is defective. Have it checked by a competent repairman, or you may ruin the filmstrip's sprocket holes.

Damage to the sprocket holes is the most frequent problem in the use of filmstrips. Unfortunately, there is no completely satisfactory means of repairing a damaged filmstrip, since the damaged section often has to be removed before the strip can be spliced. Some experts feel that the only thing that can be done with a damaged filmstrip is—make slides.

In short, a great deal of care should be taken to see that sprocket holes are not damaged.

Things To Do

Making Photographic Slides. In the mid 1950's, 2 x 2 slide making required a certain amount of photographic knowledge which the classroom teacher generally did not have. Today, simplified 35 millimeter cameras leave the user free to just push the shutter release and take the picture! With a single lens reflex camera, you can actually see what your final picture will be!

Today there appears to be little reason for using black and white film for any purpose except copy work. Color slides can give your lesson greater impact and hold pupil attention far longer. All this, at the same cost as a black-and-white positive transparency—or even less! There is a 35mm color film made for almost every condition of indoor or outdoor lighting, so there's bound to be one suitable for your purpose.

There is that one situation where black and white film is needed—copying printed or drawn matter—line copy work. Micro-File® 35mm film is used to develop extremely high contrast, which is essential in projection. However, Micro-File® needs a special development unavailable at the corner drug store. So, while you should know about its use, you'll probably have to leave the copy slide making to the local photo shop.

It's easy to see that the best slide for school use is the color transparency—and it's more effective, too.

Field Trip on 2 x 2 Slides. A field trip may be to the local fire station, the zoo, or it may be a nature walk through the park; or to any of a hundred other places. Regardless where you go, all field trips have certain essential aspects. Two of them, preparation for the trip and follow-up discussion, can be ideally covered through the use of slides. Want to try?

Make all your usual preparations for a trip—to the airport, for example. But, as part of your trip planning, add a picture "shooting script" to help you review the tour with your class.

As you decide with your pupils what you'd like to see and do on the field trip, make a list of the situations. This is your shooting script. A good way to start would be to take a shot of your pupils loading onto the bus heading for the airport. Then, a landmark or two along the bus route helps set the stage. Next, when you reach the airport, picture by slide a large sign, or the airport tower. Of course, you'll include a transparency on each of the important sights—jets, weather instruments, flight planning room, helicopters, and many more!

Be sure to "move in" close to the subject of your picture. Small images on a screen hold very little attention. They merely clutter the picture, and the desired impact is often lost. Remember, the projected image will appear far smaller than it appears to you in real life, so *move in close.*

Armed with a fine array of "shots" in your 35 mm camera, have your film processed and mounted as 2 x 2 slides. In many parts of the country, one day processing is available, so your class review and discussion can take place within a very short time after the trip itself.

The value of your slides need not stop there. They can be used as introductory materials with another class, or they may serve as a photographic field trip in themselves.

Making Photographic Lantern Slides. The 3¼ x 4 inch, or lantern slide, had all but disappeared from the educational scene, when the Polaroid Corporation developed a new type of instant print—this time formed on a transparent plastic base instead of paper. Thus Polaroid® slides were born. For teachers who want to hold class discussions about the slide immediately after the picture is taken, the Polaroid® slide is unique.

There are two types of Polaroid transparency film: one for copying line materials (outline maps, typing, etc.), and the other for continuous tone originals (people, animals, objects, multi-color art work). The line copy film (Type 147L) develops in about ten seconds; the panchromatic type takes two minutes.

Actual slide making is extremely simple. Focus the camera, release the shutter, then pull a tab to start development. After 10 seconds (or 2 minutes), remove the completed transparency from the camera. Then dip the slide in a rapid drying hardening solution and snap it into a special snap-together plastic frame. That's all there is to it—and the lantern slide is ready for use.

Photographic lantern slides can also be prepared in the darkroom by more traditional methods. Teachers who are interested in this older process may investigate it in *The Audio-Visual Handbook*.[1] The glass photographic slide explained therein no longer seems to have practical application in the classroom since other easier to use materials can provide similar results.

Handmade Lantern Slides. Most handmade slides are of the lantern size, since the smaller 2 x 2 photographic transparency has a working area of about 1½ square inches—hardly enough space for artwork! However, the lantern slide's 10 square inches of working surface will permit both tracing and artistic expression—even if to a limited degree.

If you wish to work with pencil or special translucent slide crayons,

---

[1] Ellsworth C. Dent, *The Audio-Visual Handbook* (Society for Visual Education, Inc., 327 South LaSalle Street, Chicago, Illinois, n.d.), p. 54 ff.

1— Snap it. . . .

2— Pull a tab. . . .

Fig. 1.6—Simple, quick development is the secret of the Polaroid ® slide's success. A scene can be ready for projection in a matter of just minutes after being "shot." (*Polaroid Corporation*)

3— Lift out transparency. . . .

4— Harden it. . . .

5— Mount it. . . .

6— Project it. . . .

Fig. 1.7—When doing artwork on a glass slide, a holder should always be used for greater safety.

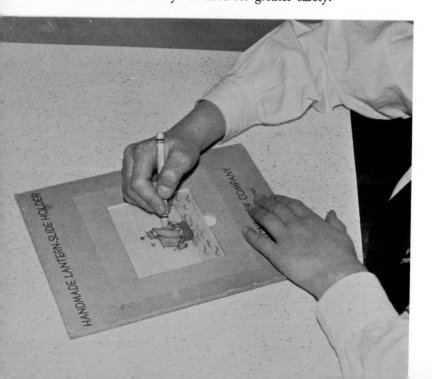

you need a frosted surface to show some "tooth" to your drawing instrument. Generally ground glass or matte surface plastic, such as
Lumarith® will provide good working characteristics. Glass, a harder
material, holds a slight advantage, however.

Middle and upper grade students have used glass slides for years,
without many reported mishaps. Nevertheless, caution should be exer-
cised since working with glass does provide a potential danger.

Making a Matte Surface Lantern Slide. Place a clean ground glass
(or matte plastic) slide in a slide holder, as shown in Fig. 1.7. This will
obviate any necessity for touching the slide—both lessening fingerprints
on the working surface and reducing potential danger, if you're working with a glass slide. The slide should first be outlined lightly in pencil,
working on the frosted surface; then, it may be colored. Originally, only
special slide crayons could be successfully used for coloring. Now, the
ever increasing variety of marking instruments being made makes it
almost impossible to be specific. Certainly slide crayons *can* be used,
but so can certain felt type pens, nylon tip pens, watercolors, pencils,
and others. The best advice is merely that the coloring medium used
must be translucent.

Clear glass slides can be used in the same manner as ground glass,
but the smooth surface demands that the art medium used be compatible with the shiny surface. The Pentel Pen® appears to work satisfactorily, as do some felt flow pens. However, it is impossible to get
even coloration when using flow pens, so slide makers should work with
the medium *as it is*, and not try to make it a medium that it *isn't*. Transparent colored paints (inks) will provide a fairly even color tone, if
that is necessary.

Formerly, coatings were placed on clear glass slides to permit them
to accept water colors. However, with the advent of translucent marking devices which *will* write on plain glass, this procedure is no longer
practical.

Lantern Slides Interpret History. One advantage found in the
lantern slide which is unavailable in the 2 x 2 photographic slide is the
ability of students to produce excellent slides with little prior experience.

One class produced an entire auditorium program about the discovery of the New World—completely on lantern slides. Each pupil
selected a different event to depict. The assignment was a simple one:
draw a slide in pencil, color it with slide crayons or translucent pencils,
and write a caption paragraph about it. Pupils were free to trace from
texts or draw original slides. One convenient factor was that most textbook illustrations were of suitable size for tracing onto slides.

When slides are to be traced from textbook illustrations, an intermediate copy will have to be made on tracing paper since there is no way to use the slide safety holder on most textbook pages.

After the ground glass slides were colored, pupils were taught to bind them with adhesive binding tape. Edge binding is essential since unbound slides could be dangerous, and a glass slide is usually bound together in a "sandwich" with a cover glass. This gives the unit enough body to be subjected to normal classroom use. In the discussion of binding and slide safety which took place in the classroom, one pupil made a suggestion which proved rather effective under test conditions. Since the shattering of a glass slide is always a possibility, one boy suggested that the glass slide be laminated together with a sheet of clear plastic coated with a pressure sensitive adhesive. He reasoned that the adhesive on the flexible acetate sheet would prevent the glass from shattering. We tried it—it worked. This seems to be a worthwhile practice, and you might want to try it with your own slides.

If Lumarith® or clear plastic is used for the slide, then you will have to bind the slide to a cover glass, for neither Lumarith® nor clear acetate will have enough body to permit its use in a projector.

Silhouette Slides. Opaque materials may be used to achieve special projection effects when using lantern slides. Cutouts of leaves, geometric shapes, and other objects can be used in teaching situations where configuration is important but where detail is unnecessary. Usually the use of silhouettes is valuable in teaching recognition, such as in the teaching of poisonous plant identification.

Cutouts are pasted to clear glass slides with rubber cement or any other suitable adhesive. Accent may be added to the background by adding a sheet of colored cellophane or acetate over the slide. Then the slide is bound together with a cover glass in the usual manner.

The same procedure may be followed with 2 x 2 slides, but the small working area is a severe problem.

Making Title and Caption Slides. The need for title and caption slides has long presented a challenge to even the most proficient audio-visualist. Commercially available slides, in the 2 x 2 size, are generally limited to "Beginning," "Intermission," and "The End." Such slides have hardly any educational value. So, the teacher must find some other means of giving a slide presentation its necessary text matter.

Probably the oldest technique used here is handwriting or printing. This may suffice for the lantern slide size, but it is of limited value with the 2 x 2 slide, since only two or three handwritten words will be able to

Fig. 1.8—Edges of slides are bound with adhesive coated slide binding tape. To bind a slide, cut a piece of tape about 15 inches long from the roll. Moisten about ½ inch of the adhesive at one end and glue the moistened tip to your working surface. Then fold the rest of the tape back so that the remaining length faces adhesive side up. Then moisten the rest of the tape and, starting from the loose end, attach the tape to the slide-cover glass sandwich as shown in the illustration, by folding the tape over both faces of the slide and simultaneously rotating the slide end-over-end, folding down the tape edges as you go along. When you reach the beginning point, allow about a ½ inch overlap, and cut off the remaining tape. Fold all corners flat against the faces of the slide.

Fig. 1.9—Silhouette slide of the poison ivy tri-leaf helps your students in identification of poisonous plants.

11

fit on the slide. Still, special 2 x 2 slides are available which will permit writing directly on the frosted surface. Or, you can make your own by inserting a sheet of Lumarith® matte acetate in a 2 x 2 mount. If you'd rather use clear plastic in the mount (and it *will* give better brilliance), just do your writing with a Pentel Pen®, or a similar fine point flow pen.

Another slide titling technique is the cellophane and carbon system. The user types onto a special carbon sheet which then offsets onto the cellophane. The imprinted cellophane is then mounted between two cover glasses and bound. While such slides are more suited to the lantern type, it has been successfully used with 2 x 2 titling also.

Carbon Ribbon Titles. A novel system of slide captioning is the use of carbon ribbon as the letter vehicle.

Many electric typewriters are equipped with mylar base carbon ribbons instead of the ink saturated cloth type found on most manual machines. This mylar ribbon is the heart of this method. To make a mylar ribbon title strip:

1. Cut a few strips of Mylar base carbon ribbon from an unused roll, and tape the strips to a sheet of paper, as shown in Fig. 1.10. The paper should be marked off to the dimension of the slide being used. For example, the maximum length of ribbon which can be used on a 2 x 2 slide is about 1¼ inches. Therefore, the guide lines must be no more than 1¼ inches apart, for any typing beyond this size will not be projected.

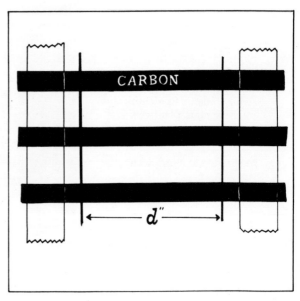

Fig. 1.10—Carbon ribbon from an electric typewriter may be used for making slide titles. "d" indicates the maximum projectable slide width for the type of slide you wish to use.

2. Insert the paper, set up as in Fig. 1.10, into any typewriter (electric preferred), and type. If you're using a manual machine, use a heavy touch, since the heavier the strike, the clearer the finished title strip will be.

3. The carbon ribbon is then removed from the paper base, and the ribbon is carefully applied to the glass slide (either 2 x 2 or 3¼ x 4).

4. Apply a cover glass, bind the edges, and project!

The carbon ribbon title strip can be applied directly to the lantern slide as a caption. However, with 2 x 2 slides you'll have to use a whole slide for the caption. If you want text material and picture on the screen, use two projectors and project picture and caption simultaneously.

Photographic Slide Titles. If you have a great deal of text material to place on a 2 x 2 or lantern slide, the only really effective means is by photography. Even without an elaborate photocopy setup, any teacher who is familiar with camera operation can make a photographic title or caption slide.

Write your text matter on a large sheet (18 x 24 inches) of white paper. Mount the paper flat on a large piece of stiff cardboard, and take it outdoors to a location with even lighting—either sun or shade. There must be no shadows cast on the paper. Next, move in as close to your subject as your 35mm camera will allow—while still giving you the entire caption you desire. Naturally, if you use color film, your text slide can be drawn in color. If you write the text matter in black and white, you would do well to use high contrast Micro-file® film, and have it developed by a photographic processor.

This method is quite suitable for the occasional text or caption transparency. However, if you want to delve extensively into photocopy work, the pamphlet, *Effective Lecture Slides,*[2] is an item of "must" reading. In it, the prospective slide maker is introduced to common errors in slide making—such as the mistaken belief that legibility of printed matter in one form (a book, for example), insures legibility in another form (transparency). Also, the pamphlet points out the fact that all too many slide makers insist on trying to cram far more material into a slide than really belongs there. How large, then, should printed matter be on a 35mm (2 x 2) transparency? Kodak says:

> If you can read 2 x 2 slides without a magnifier, people in rear seats can probably read them on the screen.

---

[2] *Effective Lecture Slides,* Sales Service Pamphlet No. S-22 (Rochester 6, N.Y.: The Eastman Kodak Company, 1963).

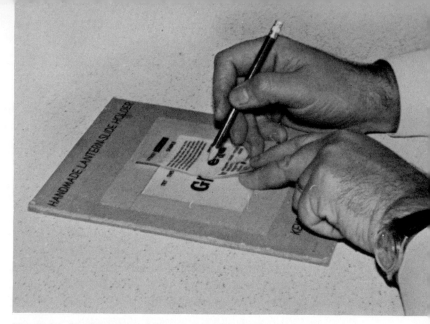

Fig. 1.11—No lettering ability is needed when you use easy to apply transfer lettering. Just burnish the desired letter on a plastic carrying sheet and the letter is instantly transferred to your slide. Both transparent and opaque letters are available. Transparent letters may be in color, but opaque letters always project black.

There is another possibility in making slides of text matter. If you have access to a Polaroid Land camera, you can use Polaroid Line Copy Transparency film to make copies of text or printed matter. However, since this film is made in sizes suited to lantern slides and 2¼ square slides, you'll have to do some trimming if the completed transparency is to fit into a 2 x 2 mount.

Titles with Press Letters. Extremely effective titles can be created on 2 x 2 and lantern slides with the use of various kinds of pre-printed press-on letters.

To use press letters merely mark off on a sheet of clear or colored acetate the area of the slide. Then, within this area, place the portion of the sheet containing the desired letter. With a ball-point pen, a pencil, or other burnishing tool, press on the plastic sheet directly over the letter. The letter will transfer to the acetate, and you then lift the sheet to select the next desired letter. Proceed in this manner through all the words you wish to place on the slide. Trim the acetate to fit your slide mount, and your press letter slide is completed. Again, if you're using 2 x 2 slides it must be remembered that this, or any other mechanical method, will severely restrict the amount of lettering which may be placed on the slide.

Making "Lift" Slides. Certain magazines, such as *Grade Teacher, National Geographic,* and *Life,* use a clay coated printing paper. Illustra-

14

tions on such stock lend themselves admirably to "lifting"—or transferring the printing ink from the page to a slide. Ease of transfer exists because the printing ink actually rests on the clay coating, not on the paper. It follows that an adhesive surface placed on the printed illustration will adhere to the ink and clay, not to the paper itself.

Very few materials are needed for making transfer slides: a burnishing tool (or teaspoon), scissors, a mild detergent solution, a cotton swab, water, slide binding tape, a clear glass lantern slide, and a sheet of clear transparent acetate coated with pressure sensitive adhesive (available in most photo or stationery shops as "laminating plastic"). The entire process of making a lift slide can be completed in less than five minutes.:

1. Peel backing from the adhesive coated side of the plastic. Place the plastic aside. Handle the plastic only by the corners and edges in order to avoid any fingerprints on the final slide.
2. Place the trimmed clipping face up on a hard, smooth surface such as plate glass (or plastic laminate). Position the plastic, adhesive side down, over the clipping, so as to have the illustration in the desired location (the center of the slide).
3. Press the plastic in contact with the clipping. To avoid air bubbles, apply pressure on one side of the plastic, then gradually lower the plastic to permit adhesion of the rest of the sheet.
4. To insure proper contact between the adhesive and the printing, rub the plastic over the printed areas with the bowl of a teaspoon (or burnishing tool). Rub until the printed matter appears perfectly clear.
5. Place the picture-plastic sandwich in lukewarm or cool water for about one minute. When the paper is *thoroughly* soaked, remove from the water.
6. Beginning at one corner, slowly pull the soaked paper away from the plastic sheet. The printing will remain on the acetate sheet.
7. Clear the clay from the adhesive by washing the slide in cool running water. A light rubbing with a cotton tipped swab dipped in a mild detergent will facilitate the clay removal.
8. After air-drying the plastic for one minute (or until all traces of water are gone), press the coated side to a piece of clear slide glass. Burnish the surface of the plastic to achieve a clear sandwich, and bind the slide.[3]

Slides made by this ink transfer method are not suitable for use with 2 x 2 slides, except for line illustrations. The enlargement given 2 x 2's is usually so great that colored illustrations appear as a tapestry-

[3] H. E. Scuorzo, "Let's Make Transfer Slides," *Grade Teacher,* Teachers Publishing Corp., February, 1961, pp. 32-33.

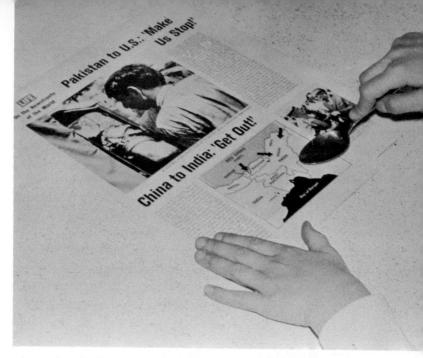

Fig. 1.12a

"Lift" slides provide the teacher with a quick, inexpensive means of making professional quality 2 x 2 or lantern slides from many magazine line illustrations. In "a," adhesive coated clear plastic

like pattern of colored dots or circles, and black-and-white halftones appear as the mass of dots which go to make up the halftone. With line copy, both 2 x 2 and lantern sizes can produce excellent lift slides.

Scratch Slides. You can make another type of slide with a specially coated plastic film. The coating is easily scratched away with a pointed stylus. The result is a slide which shows white writing against a black background.

Vu-Graph Film® can also be used to make similar transparencies on a typewriter. The film is inserted with the coated side in contact with a sheet of 9 lb. typing or tracing paper. Impression of the keys is made on the paper, not the film. As with carbon ribbon titles, the impression should be a hard, sharp one. Naturally, an electric typewriter will produce a better final slide than will a manual machine. Here too, the effect is that of white writing against a black background. In either case, the color of the writing or artwork may be varied by simply binding a sheet of colored cellophane in the slide sandwich.

Another type of scratch slide, one which permits art work, is made by spray coating a standard clear glass lantern slide with opaque lacquer or enamel. The coating must be *thin,* and it must be allowed to dry *completely* before working with it. Scratching is done with a standard mimeograph stylus; then the slide is bound in the usual way.

16

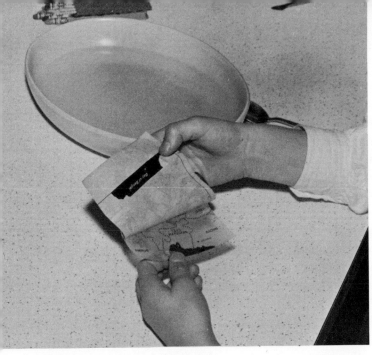

Fig. 1.12b

is burnished to the desired illustration. After being soaked in water, the (b) paper is peeled from the plastic leaving the line illustration on the slide.

Sound Slides. For the teacher who has preserved a field trip in the form of a slide show documentary, the addition of a sound track is the logical next step.

To add narration and sound effects to your presentation, you need two tape recorders. Record sound effects, appropriate to each slide, on one reel of tape. Effects may be:

1. Artificial, as the crinkling of cellophane to simulate the sound of fire crackling.
2. Live, for example the actual sound of a closing door.
3. Recorded, such as the paging system and background noise found in an airport terminal building. Recorded effects may be purchased on discs, or made locally on tape.

Locally recorded sounds in the 1950's would have been practically impossible to achieve, except on a professional, commercial basis. Today, with the art of portable tape recording at a high degree of perfection, one needs only to go out into the world armed with a portable recorder to capture the wide romance of sound available. A canary, a railroad train, a waterfall are all equally easy to capture on tape with a portable recorder (battery operated).

If it is impossible to record your sound effects in the desired order

17

of presentation, record any way you can. The incorrect order may be changed by merely cutting out the appropriate sound segments of tape and splicing them together in the proper order.[4]

Once your sound effects are in the proper order and ready to play back, you're ready to narrate your sound slides.

In a finished sound slide presentation, five separate functions must be coordinated:

1. Live narration.
2. Playing of recorded sound effects; making live and artificial ones.
3. Making a "slide advance" sound (bell, chime, cricket, etc.).
4. Projection of the slide about which the recording is being made.
5. Recording the finished tape consisting of elements 1, 2, and 3 above.

This requires teamwork if the finished recording is to be of high quality. The less you have to stop the recorder, the better your tape will be. Needless to say, *silence* must be observed by all during recording. You will be amazed to see how much extraneous sound is recorded on the tape if strict silence is not observed.

Presentations of local interest lend themselves particularly well to this treatment. Further, it is the only way sound slide presentations are available in most areas, since commercial producers restrict such items to the extensive markets of the largest cities.

Filmstrips—For Chalkboard Maps and Drawing. Teachers everywhere use the filmstrip as a projected teaching tool. But have you ever thought of it as a source of chalkboard material?

When you discover a filmstrip that has a frame which particularly interests you, just project it on your chalkboard and copy the projected picture in chalk. When you're finished copying, turn the projector off, and you'll have a chalk reproduction of the filmstrip original.

This technique is particularly useful in the social studies and science areas where maps and diagrams must be accurate, but are often difficult to draw freehand.

If you'd rather have a permanent copy for future use, try drawing on heavily sized muslin or a bristol coated chipboard. The sized muslin (or an old window shade) could be rolled up for storage. If you prefer a flat copy, the bristol "fills the bill" nicely. A flow pen is best for tracing on either of these bases.

The Projector—A Handy Light Source. Most filmstrip projectors designed for classroom use are rated at 300 watts or more. This fact

---

[4] *See* Chapter 6 for details on tape splicing.

makes the projector a valuable source of high intensity, high contrast light. And such a light source is certainly needed!

Take, for example, in geography. A teacher may try to use a flashlight to simulate the sun shining on the globe to show how day and night occurs. If you've done this, you know how inadequate a flashlight is for this purpose! But your 300 or 500 watt filmstrip or slide projector—that's another story! Its condensing lens and reflector system concentrates all the light into a narrow beam. Projected on your globe, it is relatively as bright as the sun is on the earth. If you can darken your classroom, the effect is striking, for it simulates the earth in the dark void of space more accurately.

Use of the slide projector as a light source is not limited to geography. In science instruction, a three projector light source can provide some interesting and imaginative instruction.

First, make three color slides from filter material of the three primary *light* colors. (Since the three colors which make white light are considered "primary," use filters of red, blue, and green.)

The mixing of all three primary colors of light will result in "white" light on the screen. (Note: since the color intensity and light of each projector must be in exactly the right proportion to produce pure white light, the chances are that you will actually get an "off white," affected by the dominant color of the three.) Mixing any two colors will be equally spectacular for your pupils, who are undoubtedly familiar only with the primary colors of pigments, not light!

Shadow plays are easily set up with the projector, too. A shadow play is essentially a living silhouette show.

For this you'll need a large translucent screen, the players, and a slide or filmstrip projector to use as a light source. At the start, the audience sees only a blank screen. All preparations take place behind the screen in subdued light. Since the screen is usually a white bed sheet, there's no need to worry about "see through," as long as a subdued light is used behind the screen during preparation. However, when the shadow play begins, all lights should be off except the projector. You'll need all the contrast you can get to have a good, clear shadow. The novelty of the shadow play heightens interest—and costumes are almost unnecessary.

An even simpler type of shadow play uses cardboard cutouts as actors, and is quite suited to the primary grades. Pupils standing beneath the translucent screen hold the cutouts on sticks, and move them according to the mood of the dialogue.

Good Public Relations through Slides. One of the crying needs in education is an improved ability of the school to interpret its function, methods, and success to the public. Support for your class, your school, even your district, often can be developed if you have an informed public.

The 35mm camera and the slide projector can help you do the needed job! Parents want to know what their children are doing in school, but few can spend full time observing the school in action. The slide lets you bring the school and classroom to the parents—and in color, too!

Show planning should be based on your ultimate purpose. Do you want to show a child's progress in arithmetic from grade to grade? Or are there poor facilities the public ought to know about? Did your class have a culminating activity that can show parents the ramifications of a unit of work in social studies?

You can see by these examples that P-R Topics are widely enough varied to *force* you to think: What really belongs in my program?

One caution for the teacher-photographer planning a slide show for P-R (or instructional) purposes: *If the quality of the finished transparency isn't all you want it to be, destroy it.* A blank screen can carry your message as well—or better—than a poor slide!

Avoid distant shots. They are seldom pleasing to the viewer. Instead, concentrate on what people, pupils and teachers, are doing; and be sure to move in close to the activity before shooting your picture.

A satisfied group of parents—pleased with the accomplishments of their children and the school—is the best advocate a school can have.

Using Slides and Filmstrips in the Classroom. Using a filmstrip or slide correctly involves far more than merely inserting the film and flipping on the switch.

The first step in good use is good selection. And the essential factor in good selection is "preview." You must know what it is you want to accomplish through the use of projected still pictures. Then previewing can tell you whether the material in question will really accomplish your purpose. If not, don't use it!

Your pupils must be ready to see and listen. Prepare them for the filmstrip or slides before use. Essentially, it can be summarized in the old military cliche: Tell them you're going to do it; do it; tell them what you did. While this might qualify as reducing instruction to the absurd, it is worthy of some thought.

Is your classroom ready? Is it sufficiently darkened for use? Or do you have light streaming on the screen through an expanse of glass block and window? Is the temperature comfortable and healthful? Are pupils seated so that all can see? Are you seated so that you can see all of your pupils? All are questions, but *you* must have the correct answers if you want to be ready to use slides and filmstrips!

And during actual use—what happens then? The teacher is the best judge of what should happen, provided all factors have been considered. For example, hit or miss should not determine who reads the filmstrip captions. Caption reading can be a wonderful language experience for many pupils. On the other hand, it can be absolutely devastating for the pupil unable to read the caption—either through non-selection or inability! You can do the narration, and provide proper tone and inflection. Regardless what road you select, do it for a reason that will benefit your pupils.

During projection, see to it that all possible distractions are eliminated. While the brightened screen is a magnificent attention-getting force, distractions can be present and they *can* ruin the presentation. The student who isn't paying attention derives no value from the lesson!

Above all, have a follow-up. Good advice is "Immediately following the showing of the filmstrip or slides, the viewing group should be guided in their evaluation of the material in terms of the well-defined purpose for which the material was used." [5] Discussion is the most valuable form of follow-up. In it, the teacher should elicit what understandings and information the pupils gained from both picture and caption. She should determine whether it is necessary to view the filmstrip again to gain valuable information which might have been overlooked. And, for her own purpose, she should determine whether the time spent was productive, and if it was, make a notation about the filmstrip or slide set for future use.

---

[5] A. J. Foy Cross and Irene F. Cypher, *Audio-Visual Education* (New York: Thomas Y. Crowell Company, 1961), p. 84.

Chapter Two

MOTION
PICTURES

There's no motion in a motion picture. An unusual statement? Not at all, for there really isn't any! The motion picture is but a sensory illusion, and the teacher who understands the basic principles of the illusion has a head-start in knowing and using movie equipment.

To understand the illusion, we must remember that the human eye has a quality called "persistence of vision." Simply stated, it means that whatever the eye sees, it continues to see for a fraction of a second after the stimulus is removed from view.

To illustrate, let's use a series of pictures of an arrow and a target. In each picture, the arrow is slightly closer to the target. If as few as sixteen such pictures are seen separately and in succession, in one second, the illusion would be that of a smooth motion of the arrow to the target.

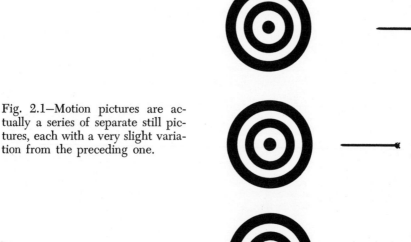

Fig. 2.1—Motion pictures are actually a series of separate still pictures, each with a very slight variation from the preceding one.

22

Naturally, the more pictures used per second, the smoother the "motion" will be.

When these closely related actions are placed on a transparent plastic base, we have motion picture film. The device used to project the film must be capable of flashing a picture on a screen, blacking it out, and then showing the next picture in as little as a fiftieth of a second. Persistence of vision will blend the separate flashed pictures into a "motion" picture.

Motion Picture Equipment

Motion Picture Film. Two widths of motion picture film are in school use—16 millimeter and 8 millimeter. By far, the more common size is 16mm. Hardly a school can be found without a 16mm sound projector. Most commercially produced educational films are made in the 16mm size. Eight millimeter film is making inroads in the local production field. Another common American size, 35mm, is seldom used in schools, and even when it is, it is only for the largest auditorium use. It will, therefore, not be considered in this book in regard to its motion picture use.

16MM. The vast majority of 16mm educational films are sound films. Silent 16mm film is easily distinguished from the sound variety by the dual sprocket holes found on silent film; sound film is perforated on only one edge, and the sound track is along the other.

While it is the rare school which owns a 16mm *silent* projector, a caution is still in order. *Never attempt to thread sound film into a projector intended only for silent film.* Since sound film has but one set of sprocket holes, using it in a silent machine, which has *two* sets of sprocket teeth, *always* ruins the film. *Sound* projectors, on the other hand, are

Fig. 2.2–Sixteen millimeter film

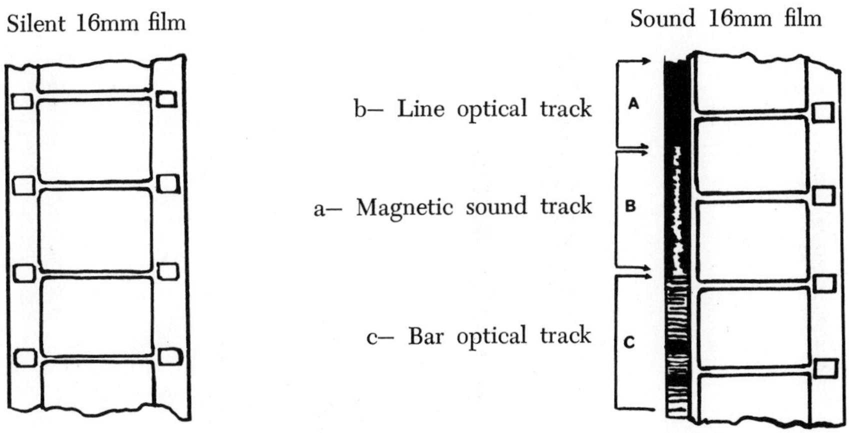

Silent 16mm film

Sound 16mm film

b— Line optical track   A

a— Magnetic sound track   B

c— Bar optical track   C

designed for using both sound and silent films; but when silent films are run, one set of sprocket holes remains unused.

Educational film producers often make film available in both color and black-and-white. The cost of 16mm color prints is substantially higher than BW, and your school should consider this fact when purchasing a film *if* color is not an essential element of the subject. If it is, price should not be allowed to be a limiting factor. You'd do better not to purchase the film at all. Wait until the budget will allow for that which fills the instructional need.

Sixteen millimeter film is wound on a basic 400 foot reel, with a running time of approximately 11 minutes for sound film, and 16 minutes for silent. At first, this might seem unusual—two different running times for the same length of film—but there's a reason. Sound film runs at a faster rate than silent. It moves past the lens at a rate of 24 frames per second, as opposed to 16 for silent. Although the reason for the increased speed was based mainly on sound quality requirements, it has resulted in better visual quality too—less flicker, a better illusion of motion.

If you want to estimate the running time of 16mm film, you can do it by remembering the 11 and 16 minute base times for one 400 foot reel. Since reels are made in multiples of 400 feet, and are marked at every 100 feet, you should be able to estimate the footage and the running time. If you work on a period schedule, running time takes on tremendous importance.

8MM. For more than three decades, 8mm film was really 16mm film which had been double perforated and split down the middle during processing. The result was a film 8mm wide with a single row of perforations along one edge. It was made to conform with 16mm characteristics (as sprocket hole size) and was not a design of its own.

Fig. 2.3—The sound track area is shown by a black strip. Format M as shown can have either an optical or magnetic track. Present Super 8, Double Super 8, and Standard 8 all use magnetic tracks.

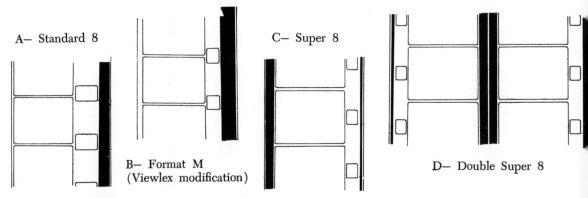

A— Standard 8

C— Super 8

B— Format M
(Viewlex modification)

D— Double Super 8

In early 1965, the Eastman Kodak Company announced that it would market a completely new 8mm film—only the width remained the same. The new film, Super 8, provides fifty per cent more picture area than the standard 8mm film. The height and width of each frame (individual picture) have been increased to provide this added area. More light can therefore be transmitted through each frame, so the projected image is substantially brightened. A double Super 8 film was introduced late in 1965, but its use will probably be limited to offerings of commercial film producers. Like the standard double 8, it must be slit down the middle after development since it is 16mm wide in its original form.

Another 8mm design, Format M, was modified and used by the Viewlex Corporation as the basis for a semi-automatic threading projector. The projector's design enables it to project the modified Format M film with a magnetic or optical sound track, in addition to any standard 8mm sound or silent film. The projection area of this modified Format M film is sixteen per cent larger than standard 8. This is considerably less than the fifty per cent increase offered by Super 8, but this format does provide *optical* sound. It could be the key to an 8mm revolution, especially as cartridge loading full length 8mm sound projectors are introduced.

Commercially produced 8mm educational sound films and projectors sell for approximately one-half the price of similar 16mm equipment.

This incipient revolution was a long time in the making. For decades 8mm film was hardly more than a curiosity in school use. However, in the early 1960's, educators began experimenting with 8mm for small group and individual instruction. The success of their experiments, and the entry into the educational field of a major film producer with a new idea, cartridge projection, gave the needed impetus.

The Project on Educational Communications suggests a variety of production categories for the 8mm user. Although the categories are not exhaustive, and other uses will probably be developed, some of the immediate areas are: "(1) Moving Illustrations, (2) Documentaries, (3) Skill Films, (4) Drill Films, (5) Context Films, (6) Visualized Abstractions, (7) Induction or Deduction Films, (8) Story Films, and (9) Hybrid Still/Motion Films." [1]

Motion Picture Sound. Most instructional film is 16mm wide and contains a sound track. Most 8mm film does not have a sound track, but very easily could have one. Only two methods of sound reproduction are used in ordinary motion pictures—optical and magnetic. Both 8 and

[1] Louis Forsdale, Joan Rosengren Forsdale and John Swayze, "A Point of View" in *8: Newsletter of 8mm Film in Education*, No. 1, March 1965, pp. 2-3.

16mm may be equipped with both tracks. When this is done, each track is usually suited to a different audience, either by treatment of subject matter or by the use of different languages.

In the optical system, sound is converted into electrical impulses, then to light, which is impressed photographically on the film. The optical track is visible as a wavy line or series of shaded bars along one edge of the film. To reproduce the sound, a finely focused beam of light from an exciter bulb is shone through the sound track. This causes a varying beam of light to fall on a photoelectric cell. The cell produces electrical variations in the same pattern as the light. These electrical variations are then amplified and converted into sound.

Magnetic track (stripe) operation is quite similar. Live sounds are again converted into electrical impulses. But then they are changed into magnetic variations which are recorded invisibly onto a stripe of iron oxide, like that found on recording tape. Reproduction is the reverse. The invisible magnetic sound pattern alignment on the stripe is "read" by a magnetic coil, or "head," converted into electrical impulses and finally into sound.

Magnetic sound is well suited to local production since recording on film is no different from making an ordinary tape recording. An optical track, however, is largely restricted to professional productions, and is definitely not suited to local production use by the classroom teacher or pupils.

Motion Picture Camera. The motion picture camera is nothing but a device to take a series of still photographs in rapid succession. Since 16mm cameras are the tools of professional and semi-professional cameramen, they need not be treated here. Eight millimeter cameras are for the teacher and pupil to use, so let's look at some of the basic camera characteristics.

Most have a battery drive which transports the film through the camera without winding. Even spring wound cameras now have a very long running time in order to minimize the possibility of having to rewind mid-scene. Exposure control is automatic; a photo-sensitive cell acts as a light meter and sets the lens at the proper opening. "Zoom" type lenses have eliminated lens changing for different shots, and will allow for a closeup or for distant scenes at the push of a button or lever. Less expensive cameras have a universal focusing which will give acceptable pictures under most conditions of distance; better cameras provide for critical focusing from about 3 feet to infinity, for the sharpest possible scenes. Film loading is simple too. Most standard double 8's and *all* Super 8 cameras feature magazine loading. You never touch the film itself.

Fig. 2.4—Cartridge loading cameras make it impossible to accidentally spill or unreel film during loading. (*Eastman Kodak Company*)

Fig. 2.5—New automatic loading projectors need only to have the film inserted at the proper place. Then the machine takes over and does the threading for you! (*Bell & Howell Company*)

The simplicity of modern motion picture cameras can be summed up in one purposeful oversimplification: Point the camera and push the button.

But as automatic as they are, one major area remains for the teacher—the most important one! Cameras can't plan your film. You'll have to do that yourself!

Motion Picture Projector. Not too many years ago, some teachers felt that a master's degree in audiovisual education was needed to thread a projector; to operate one certainly required a doctorate! An exaggeration? Perhaps. But many teachers still feel that way!

Actually, there's little reason for such apprehension. The motion picture projector of today is a well engineered device designed to operate with a minimum of difficulty. It projects pictures in rapid succession,

27

draws the film past the sound head or drum, and winds the film onto the takeup reel after use.

In recent years, conventional projectors, both 8 and 16 millimeter, have turned to automatic threading in order to lessen teacher fears about using motion pictures. Automatic loading projectors require only the insertion of film into a slot—whereupon the machine takes over and guides the film into sprockets, film gate, sound drum, and in some cases, even onto the takeup reel!

Showing Motion Pictures

The teacher who would use motion pictures for instruction must have three equipment essentials: adequate light control, a suitable projector, and a projection screen. Ideally, film should be shown in the classroom, for motion pictures are a part of instruction, not something in addition to it. The use of so-called "visual aid" rooms, while often a necessary expedient, is unfortunate.

Satisfactory room darkening can be achieved in most classrooms by using opaque shades, blinds or drapes. Every effort should be made to have full light control equipment in each schoolroom.

Selection of a suitable projector involves some factors about which the teacher should be concerned:

a. Picture and sound quality.
b. Ease of operation.
c. Ease of emergency lamp and belt replacement.
d. Frequency of film damage.

The Screen. In the ideal classroom, there will be a wall mounted or pull-down screen ready for instant use. The surface will be matte white, glass beaded, silver, or lenticular. There may also be a translucent rear view screen available.

The matte white screen gives the widest viewing angle, and is especially useful when the audience must be seated unusually close to the screen. It gives maximum resolution at short distances. Since the matte screen is used for close viewing, its relatively poor reflective ability, or "brightness," is of little importance. However, if a matte screen is used for long viewing distances, especially with color projection, its lack of brightness becomes a serious drawback.

Beaded screens are quite common in audiovisual use today. This

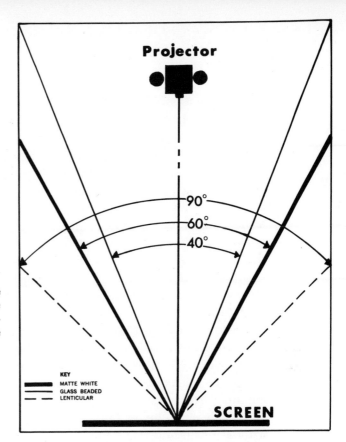

Fig. 2.6—Persons seated within the viewing arcs for a particular type screen will be able to see the projected image without objectionable brightness loss.

type has a much greater reflective power than the matte screen, but the brightness is greatest on the projection axis and drops off rapidly to a level which, beyond 30 degrees from the axis, is inadequate.

The smooth silver screen is well suited to color reproduction for its metallic particles emphasize colors and increase brightness above the level of the matte white screen. Viewing angle and brightness are slightly less than modern types of beaded screens.

The best screen surface developed to date is the lenticular. Lenticulation may be embossed in a vertical or horizontal direction, or in both. They're expensive, but they do combine good color quality, high reflectivity, and a fairly wide viewing angle (96 to 100°). There is virtually no loss of light at any viewing angle within the range. The maximum usable angle for this screen is determined not by its reflectivity, but rather by the point at which distortion occurs (due to the lenticular surface).

In some applications, particularly in a lighted classroom, projection through a translucent screen is more practical than the reflective method, since it gives greater image brightness. Translucent rear projection screens are generally made of ground glass or plastic.

29

Ventilation. One of the most obvious necessities in any room with a large number of people is ventilation. Yet, during projection, this simple health necessity is often overlooked! The least satisfactory solution is opening the windows since this can be accompanied by the blowing of shades or blinds. The best answer is a forced air or ventilating system. Since the teacher has no control over the latter method, the only practical suggestion is that ventilation be kept even. Try to have open windows as far away from the screen surface as possible. Light from blown shades or drapes might be endured at the rear of the room, but when it falls on the screen surface it can be the ultimate distracting influence!

Cartridge Projectors. From the early 1960's, educators began using 8mm film in small group instruction. The advent of Super 8 made it obvious that 8mm was suitable for classroom use too. But the factor that removed 8mm from the curio shelf and placed it in the classroom was the development of the inexpensive closed loop cartridge projector. By 1965 there were already over 1400 cartridge loops produced by educational film makers, and it was evident that the increase would be in the hundreds each year.

Each cartridge contains an amount of film which runs continuously without rewinding. Most hold only 50 feet of film, but a few contain as much as 400 feet, or about 30 minutes running time, both in sound and silent types.

The most popular form of cartridge projection, and the one most suited to local production, is the short 4 minute loop containing about 50 feet of 8mm or Super 8 film. As originally conceived by Technicolor, cartridge projection was of the "single concept" variety. It soon became apparent that the system could be used to present film ideas which

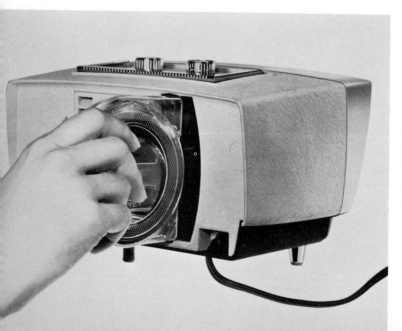

Fig. 2.7—Even the threading is eliminated with the cartridge projector. Just insert the factory loaded cartridge, flip the switch, and project! (*Technicolor Corporation, Commercial & Educational Division*)

hardly qualified as "single concept," but which could be adequately presented in the available 4 minutes. Teachers realized that these film loops could be individually used by students while other pupils did different tasks. A new media was born.

Plan for Film Use. All too often, some teachers merely "show movies." It's an easy trap in which to fall, and it is unintentionally encouraged by some administrators who feel that the use of the motion picture projector must be scheduled. You're really caught in it when you think, "I'm scheduled, so I might as well use the time."

So you proceed to use a film as an entertainment movie rather than as an instructional film. Of course, it's not intentional, but the result is the same as if it were! Film should be used for some educational purpose which you have clearly in mind, not merely for entertainment value.

This is not to say that certain films produced primarily for entertainment purposes might not have a completely justified school use. They certainly might, and often do! The key to the question of proper film use lies in what you hope to achieve and what the pupils gain by using the film.

Certain suggestions are necessary for any teacher who uses a film as an instructional tool:

1. Preview it. If you wouldn't try to use a textbook which you hadn't read, don't try it with a film. The preview will help you determine just what facts, concepts, and understandings you want your students to get from the film.
2. Show only those films which relate to class work. There's little justification for any others in the classroom.
3. Prepare pupils for the film. Before you show it, discuss with the class some of the points you expect the students to learn. It will give them a reason for watching. (There are exceptions to this, especially when you're using impact or reaction films.)
4. Show only what you need. If only 5 minutes of a 25 minute film is related to your work, use only the 5 minute portion.
5. Don't think you have to project the entire film at one time. If there's a reason to stop the projector, do so. Sometimes this is necessary to help immediate recall of a particular point on the film. Even show it over again if needed. It should be remembered, however, that the stop-film technique can be over-used, so use it thoughtfully and wisely.
6. Evaluate the film after use. If your pupils have not learned from the film, its use has been a mere waste of time. Oral evaluation may serve, as may a written quiz—especially if the pupils are forewarned about the evaluation.

THINGS TO DO

Write Script. The first step in writing any script is planning. To begin, ask yourself, "What do I want this film to do, say, or show?" or "What is my purpose?" Write down the answer. Then re-write until your intent is so clear that there's no possibility of deviating. By that time you'll have delimited your subject enough to plan and write a story which will achieve your purpose.

When you've completed the story, you're ready to "put the words to music"—to write the script for camera. The script is actually a direction sheet for shooting your film. It's usually prepared in two columns, with picture information on the left and sound information on the right. The picture column includes the scene, type of shot (closeup, distant, moving in, etc.), camera directions, and a description of the actors and their movements. In the sound column, put the narration, dialogue, and sound effects directions. If you plan only a silent film, then only the picture column will be needed.

When your script is finished, re-read it to make certain that it is clear, and that you have provided for any necessary transition from one scene to another (as a title frame, a fade out-fade in, etc.).

Take the Pictures. After you've completed the scenario, determine what film you'll need for the camera you've selected. Since you'll probably be working with an 8mm size, your selection will be limited to the amateur film available. Although 8mm sizes do not have the wide array of emulsions and speeds which are available to professionals in 16mm sizes, the film should be quite satisfactory. Unless there is an overriding reason for using black-and-white, try shooting in color.

A few simple rules can help to conserve film and time, and make your shooting easier:

1. Follow the instructions found with every camera and every roll of film.

2. Take heed of your light conditions. Most color film is balanced for either artificial light of various types or for daylight (at noon plus or minus 2 hours). Use a good exposure meter if your camera doesn't have an electric eye lens diaphragm. Light levels are most difficult for even a professional to approximate.

3. Keep your lens clean using a lintless cloth or a lens tissue. *Don't* use silicone impregnated eyeglass lens tissue, as the silicone may destroy the lens coating.

4. Make certain the drive battery is in good condition before shooting. If the camera is a winding type, wind it fully before each scene.

5. Keep the camera steady. If you can mount it on a sturdy tripod, do so. Most of the "bouncing," so characteristic of amateur work, is due to hand-held cameras.

6. Take your time! Unless you're going in for subliminal instruction, plan to have your subject on the screen long enough for it to have the desired effect on the viewer. If a title is the subject, two or three seconds might be enough; but if it's an action scene involving people, animals, or mechanical movement—8 to 10 seconds is generally regarded as a minimum. No absolute guides are possible; scene length depends on your intended effect. It is possible to shoot a scene too long, but this is seldom the hallmark of the beginner!

7. When your scenes involve rapid action, shoot them at about a 30 degree angle, with the action moving *toward* the camera. Pictures of action moving laterally past the camera lens end up as a sideways smear when projected.

8. Avoid "panning." Moving the camera laterally to get a sweeping view of an essentially non-motion scene should be left to the professional. The effect is quite similar to that suggested in No. 7 above, except that in too rapid panning the whole scene is blurred, not merely the moving object.

9. When taking outdoor pictures, don't let the sun shine into your camera lens. Light should be on the action, not the camera. Pictures taken with the sun shining into the camera (or at the rear of the subject) invariably result in overexposure or in heavily backlighted subjects which appear as mere silhouettes.

10. Use variations from normal speed only when absolutely necessary. Film should generally be shot at the same speed at which it will be projected (16 frames for double 8 and 16mm silent; 18 frames for Super 8 silent; 24 frames for 8 and 16mm sound).

Edit the Film. After your film has been processed by a commercial laboratory, the next task you face is editing. Seldom will anyone "shoot" a length of film which has no poorly photographed, poorly acted, or improperly timed sequences. You may have to delete parts which, upon viewing, seem out of place in the production. Regardless what the reason may be, editing is always needed.

An essential piece of equipment in proper editing is an "action editor," a device which shows you your film as it will appear when pro-

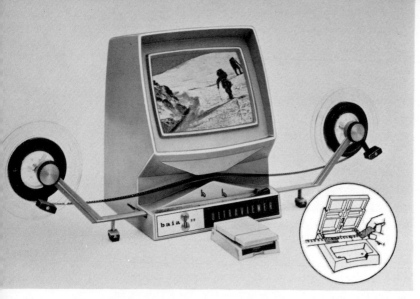

Fig. 2.8—The action editor lets you view the film you've taken as it will appear on the screen. When you reach a section you want to edit out, just remove the film from the editor and insert it in the splicer (see inset). Modern pressure sensitive adhesive splices make film editing an easy task. (*Baia Corporation*)

jected, and allows you to stop whenever you need to cut or splice film sections.

The teacher who shoots and edits his own film has a problem. Pride of authorship often causes a sequence to be included when almost any independent editor would have let it drop to the cutting room floor! With this caution firmly in mind, you're ready to splice.

There are two kinds of splices which you will use—"butt" and "overlap." If your film is used in a cartridge projector or some automatic loaders, butt splices *must* be used. If it is one of the new polyester base plastics, butt splices are essential. If it is not in either of these categories, the overlap splice will generally suffice.

In butt splicing, the two pieces of film to be joined are precisely cut so that they match, or butt, each other, while aligning perfectly with the sprockets on the splicer. The special splicing tape is then applied, and burnished down to complete the splice.

To make an overlap splice, the film ends are again precisely cut, but about ⅛ inch overlap is provided. The emulsion is scraped from one side of the film to be spliced, and the other side is roughened. Film cement is applied to the overlap, and the splice is clamped together until the bond becomes secure.

Add Sound to Your Motion Pictures. Most 16mm school projectors are equipped for optical sound; some are designed for both optical and magnetic. All 8mm formats can be provided with magnetic sound; some optical and some magnetic.

If you choose to add sound to your 8mm film, it will undoubtedly be magnetic. The initial step is applying an iron oxide sound stripe to one edge of the film. Super 8 film will also have a balance stripe along the opposite side of the film to provide for balanced winding on the film reel. While you can purchase equipment to add the stripe, commercial film processors are much better equipped to do it than you can ever hope to be. Have your sound stripe applied during film processing, and you'll be rewarded in better sound quality.

Narration is the easiest sound to add to film, for it can be done by merely speaking into the recording microphone during projection.

One caution must be observed during narration recording. The microphone should not be allowed to pick up the sound of the running projector. Often this will be difficult, since microphone cords are generally only 3 to 6 feet long, and the addition of a microphone extension would only serve to reduce sound quality. Record from the location which, after testing, gives the least objectionable background noise.

To prepare for narration, view your completely edited film while you have pencil and paper in hand. Time each sequence in seconds, and list the length of time each takes. Then plan your narration to fit the available time. As easy as a narration track is to prepare, you may still have the problem of preventing the narration for one scene from running into another scene. The solution is as simple as it is obvious. Make your narration shorter than the scene. Then, if you begin speaking when the scene starts, you'll probably finish on time.

If you wish, you can write your narration in a non-specific manner. Then it will be general enough to carry from scene to scene without creating a problem.

Try not to fall into the novice trap of telling the viewer exactly what he's seeing. The script should relate closely to the motion picture, but in such a way that the visual impression is reinforced by the commentary in a manner which doesn't appear condescending. For example, if your scene is of a penguin in a zoo cage, your commentary should not be, "This is a penguin in a zoo cage." That fact should be obvious to the viewer. Try instead, "The penguin's native habitat is the frozen Antarctic continent. When in captivity, he enjoys having blocks of ice in his cage."

Music can be added simultaneously by having an assistant play the desired background from tape or record at the proper moment. This requires a good deal of practice. Coordination is essential, for the music and narration must be in proper volume proportions. If your projector has an earphone monitoring jack, listen while recording, since it is the only way you can get the desired sound balance between background music and narration.

Super 8 film has some advantages over standard double 8 when it comes to recording, too. Although both use the same number of frames per second, the Super 8 frame is taller, and consequently the same number of frames uses a greater amount of film. It is therefore moving past the sound head at a greater speed than standard 8. As mentioned earlier, the more rapid the speed, the better the potential for quality recording. In addition, Super 8 has a narrow oxide coating, called a balance stripe, on the edge opposite the sound stripe. This stripe may some day be used as a timing or cueing strip or even for another, though lower quality, sound track—if manufacturers make equipment capable of using it!

Prevent Film Damage. Motion picture film can be damaged in many ways. As far as the teacher is concerned, four facets of the problem are important:

1. What type of film damage might occur, and how to prevent it.
2. Emergency measures for repairing film breaks or damage during projection.
3. Repair of your own film, or repair of a borrowed or rental film which must be used again for another showing.

The common damages which can occur are sprocket holes, silent projector damage to sound film, breaks or tears, and scratches.

Fig. 2.9—Types of film damage. To safeguard the rest of the film, all damaged segments, except type 3, should be spliced out of the reel.

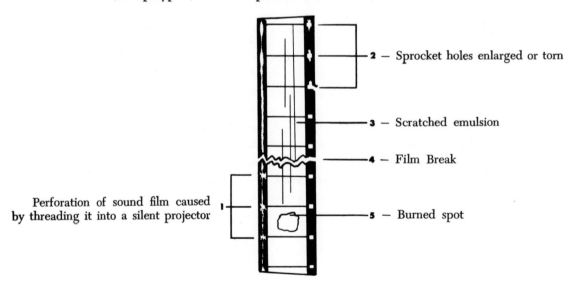

2 — Sprocket holes enlarged or torn

3 — Scratched emulsion

4 — Film Break

Perforation of sound film caused by threading it into a silent projector

5 — Burned spot

Improper threading generally causes the first damage to sprocket holes; the rest just happens. Sprocket hole damage can be easily identified during projection by the "bumping blur" and the loss of film loop above or below (usually below) the film gate. The blur is an indication that the film is not being pulled past the lamp at exactly the right moment because the sprocket holes are enlarged or ripped. Poor projection equipment can damage sprocket holes too. If your film seems to have a great many problems of this type, send the projector out for repair.

Film with sprocket hole damage should not be run through the projector. It will only serve to extend the damage along a greater length of film. Rather, report the damage to the library from which you secured the film. Caught early, such damage can be contained.

Breaks or tears caused by a faulty projector, or "green" film, or old, brittle film obviously can't be prevented by the teacher. However, the projector that breaks film should be taken out of service and given an immediate checkup.

If a film breaks during projection and you wish to continue the lesson, here's a trick that will allow you to do so. Let about 3 or 4 feet of film to run free through the projector. Then take the loose end of the film on the takeup reel and unwind 3 to 4 feet from it. Place the loose end of film from the projector on the takeup reel, and, while holding it tightly to the film already on the reel, turn the takeup reel slowly to rewind both the film you have unwound and the loose end of film from the projector. If the rewound film is tight enough, it will hold the end of the film from the projector, and you may begin again.

To some, this may appear complicated, but it is the *only* accepted method. *Do not tape film pieces together.* In addition to the possible damaging effect of the tape itself, a taped film can be severely ripped during unknowing projection.

Of course, if a broken film is your own property, or if it must be used before return to its source, splicing may be necessary. Splicing methods are discussed on page 113. If you splice a rental or borrowed film in an emergency, always notify the source that you have done so and tuck a piece of paper in the film at the point of the splice so that the film library can easily check your work.

Produce a Cartridge Film. The most practical first attempt at local production should probably be a 4 minute cartridge film. Script writing for a 10 to 30 minute feature is a tremendous task, so it's better to grow into it!

Simple tasks which lend themselves to solely visual presentation are ideal for short loops. They may be parts of a series which depict a larger process, or they may be totally independent topics. An example of the former is seen in this commercially produced series of 4 minute cartridges: [2]

Series:	Ski Techniques
Topics:	Preliminaries
	Walking
	Climbing
	Straight Running

There are 16 more such limited topics. It is obvious that each ski technique, at least for instructional purposes, must be treated separately though they are all part of one major subject.

The individual short subject is exemplified by a film such as *Using Your Toothbrush*,[3] a short loop designed to show children the proper method of toothbrush use.

In the primary grades, short loops could be used to show community helpers actually at work in neighborhood settings. Other topics might be "How to Use a Scissors," "Manuscript Letter Formation," "Birds in Our Neighborhood," and hundreds of others. Middle grade loops might cover plant growth, principles of magnetism, local government, industries and occupations, and subjects of local interest.

Here's a sample of the type of simple shooting script that could be developed for a local production:

Community Helpers

Scene	Shooting Time
1. Title: Community Helpers	3 sec.
2. Sub-Title: The Policeman	3 sec.
3. Child leaves home and walks down street toward school (view at home, rear view walking).	20 sec.
4. Child approaches corner where policeman directs traffic (rear shot then switch to front).	15 sec.
5. Switch to traffic light. Show light change to red.	10 sec.
6. Policeman puts hand up as sign to stop (distant shot, then zoom in to pick up head and hand).	10 sec.
7. Children wait at crosswalk. Show red light in shot; also patrols with arms extended.	15 sec.

The rest of the scenes could be planned in the same manner. Each succeeding scene should closely relate to the preceding one so that the

---

[2] Scope Productions (Fresno, California).
[3] Avis Films (Burbank, California).

continuity will be immediately evident. Remember, most cartridge loops have no sound to aid with continuity. The pictures must do the job alone!

In another application, one teacher had wearied of repeatedly showing pupils how to make and use papier-mâché for various geography projects. But since *showing* was an essential part of the operation, the duplicated instruction sheet she prepared did not completely explain the task. Then she made a loop film, showing the steps in making mâché and using it in the construction of a land form model. From then on no personal demonstration time was needed. Pupils take the loop cartridge to a projection corner, and learn by seeing the process done on film.

Make a Substitute Projection Screen. There's little doubt about it; a commercially manufactured screen performs best. But if you get a thrill from trying to make something yourself, or if you just can't get a manufactured screen, here are three ideas you can try:

1. Matte White Screen. In an emergency, all you need do to get a satisfactory matte white screen is turn around the roll-up wall map found in most upper elementary and high school classrooms. The back is usually white. Pull it down, and there's your screen.

2. Silver Screen. This is almost as simple. Secure a large sheet of cardboard or other smooth surface material about the size of the projection screen you want. Spray it with an aluminum aerosol spray enamel. When it dries, you have an excellent surface for color projection. We even know of one teacher who sprayed on unused chalkboard area and made a permanent screen!

3. Rear Projection Screen. (a) First make a suitable rectangular wooden frame. Pre-cut frame members, using a rabbet joint at the corners for needed strength, are generally available at mill or cabinet supply houses. Plastic white glue may be used to glue the corners together. A few brads driven through the corner joints will prevent motion while the glue is setting. (b) Purchase a sheet of translucent optical quality Celanese Acetate, .020 inches thick or more, with one side matte finished and one side polished. This plastic should be available at art supply or plastic houses. (c) Next, cut the plastic sheeting to the outer frame dimensions. Use care not to mar the matte surface of the plastic. Any fingerprints or oil stains may be removed with carbon tetrachloride, but scratches cannot be removed. (d) After the plastic sheet has been trimmed to size, place it, matte side facing up, on top of the frame. Staple or tack the plastic to the frame. Be careful to keep the semi-rigid plastic as flat as possible while attaching it, since a ripple in the screen surface

could distort the projected image. (e) Attach shelf brackets to the screen to provide a self contained stand. In the case of oblong screens, one of the longer sides should be the base. If folding shelf brackets are used, the screen can be easily stored when not in use.[4]

Remember that projection through a rear projection screen (when using motion pictures) must be reversed by reflection from a mirror so that the projected image won't appear backward to the viewer. Rear projection screens generally give enough brilliance to permit viewing in normal room illumination.

[4] H. E. Scuorzo, "Let's Make a Rear Projection Screen," *Grade Teacher*, Teachers Publishing Corp., May 1963, pp. 17 and 74. (Adapted.)

Chapter Three

OVERHEAD PROJECTION

The overhead projector won't replace the teacher; it's not intended to! Rather, it's a teaching tool which must be used *by* an instructor.

And it's one of the simplest visual devices you can use, too! Switch it on, tilt the image to the correct height, focus, and you're ready to teach —all in the space of 15 seconds.

The Projector

Simplicity is not the overhead's greatest virtue. For that, we turn to its characteristics as an instructional aid. With this projector you *face* your students in a *lighted* room. A close-to-the-screen optical system, plus an efficient light source combine to give you a large, bright image which is adequate under most normal room lighting conditions.

Fig. 3.1—The primary advantage of the overhead projector is obvious— the teacher can face her students at all times, yet she is able to point out specific details about the visual in use. (3 M Company)

41

You'll find the overhead even more effective if you dim room lights to about half their usual level. Colors appear brighter and more vivid, but you can still gain the added dimension of pupil reaction to your lesson. Facially expressed questions can be answered, even though they were never uttered! In short, the overhead projector places you in eye-contact with your pupils, and thus in instructional control of your class even during projection! And there's an advantage for students, too, for note-taking is easy in a lighted classroom.

An important factor in the overhead's usefulness is its horizontal "stage." The stage is that part of the optical system on which the transparency is placed. It serves also as a desk type "chalkboard." Everything you write on it becomes immediately visible to your students. A variety of other materials can be used on the stage also, and many of these will be covered later in this chapter.

Principles of Operation. Two types of overhead projectors are in use today. The best known type (see diagram) has its light source be-beneath the stage.

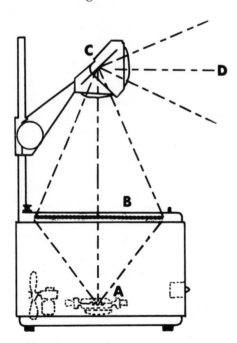

Fig. 3.2—Overhead projectors can provide brilliant images since the optical system employs a light beam which shines directly through the transparency. (A) Light source, (B) Stage where transparency is placed, (C) Projector head, and (D) Light beam to the screen. (*Charles Beseler Co.*)

Light shines through the stage (and the transparency you place on it) to the projector "head." The head contains a mirror which changes the direction of the light beam and projects the image onto the screen.

The second type is a small, light weight projector which was introduced by the 3M Company in 1965. This overhead has its light source in the head. Light shines *down*, through the transparency, to a substage mirror. From the mirror it is reflected back to the head, but at a slightly different angle. Then another mirror in the head reflects the beam onto the screen. This OHP is only adequate for use with small groups.

Portability. As originally conceived, the overhead projector was a bulky, heavy, expensive device which was best recommended for permanent, tilted installation as part of the teacher's desk. And for good reason! This was one machine which could hardly be called "portable"!

But modern machines have been reduced tremendously in size, weight and fragility through the use of lighter, more compact optical systems and high brilliance lamps. Some new portable projectors have twice the lumen output of their World War II vintage ancestors—at a third the weight! And even better lamps are on the way!

Sizes. Overhead projector size is stated in two terms—stage dimensions and lumen output.

Some manufacturers still stress wattage, but this is unfortunate, for the power expressed in watts is relatively meaningless. What you should look for is maximum lumen output delivered to the screen. Much energy of the stated wattage is dissipated in heat—especially in incandescent light sources. A 600 watt quartz-iodine lamp may well be able to deliver more light to the screen than a 1000 watt incandescent projection bulb. And the future seems even more promising!

The other size factor, stage dimensions, is rapidly becoming standardized. True, a great many 5″ x 5″ and 7″ x 7″ stage projectors are in use, but in new purchases, the 10″ x 10″ upsurge has many causes. The one most important to teachers is this: Many pictures, and a great deal of printing in books and periodicals, are suited in size to direct transfer to 10″ x 10″ transparencies by simple copy methods.

Focusing. To obtain a clear image from a good transparency, the image must be brought into sharp focus. Two methods are generally used—moving the objective lens toward or away from the screen, or, more commonly, changing the distance of the projector head from the transparency. Once focused in a particular position, there is no further need for adjustment.

Keystoning. All may be light when using the overhead, but all is not joy. Close-to-the-screen projection does give a large, bright image—but it also brings with it an optical distortion known as "keystoning." Fortunately, keystoning can be corrected.

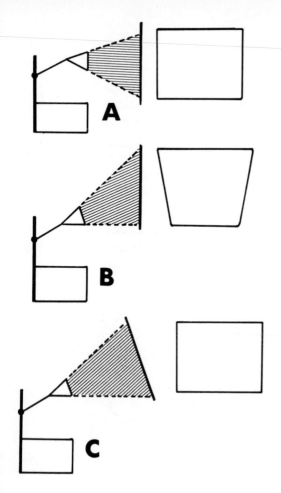

Fig. 3.3A—When the projector head is pointed directly at the screen (at an angle of 90 degrees between the light beam and the screen surface), the image appears in correct proportion. However, this is impractical except for small group use since the center of the projected image will only be at the height of the projection head. The height of the projection head is determined by the highest point at which the stage can be conveniently located.

Fig. 3.3B—When the head is tilted up to raise the image so the whole class may see, the image becomes a keystone, i.e., the top of the image is enlarged more than the bottom and distortion is caused.

Fig. 3.3C—To correct keystoning, the screen must be tilted. The image will then appear in normal proportions and the height will be convenient for viewing.

Fig. 3.4A—Ordinary screens do not provide the variable tilt needed for overhead projection. An inexpensive specialized screen shown here provides permanent classroom mounting and is adjustable for all types of projection. (*Tecnifax Corporation*)

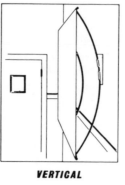

VERTICAL

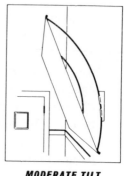

MODERATE TILT

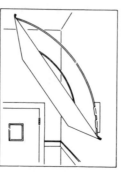

EXTREME TILT (40°)

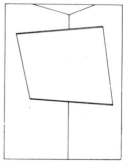

CORNER MOUNTING

44

When the projector head face and the screen are in the same plane (3.3a), projected image is normal.

With the projector head tilted up to place the image high enough for all students to see all of it, keystoning occurs (3.3b).

The use of a raised, tilted screen can cure keystoning since tilting the screen's top edge forward can restore the head's face and the screen to the same plane.

If you intend to use an overhead projector frequently, you should consider an inexpensive wall mounted tilting screen, such as that shown in Fig. 3.4. This screen can readily be adjusted for other applications where keystone correction is not a factor.

Fig. 3.4B—The ideal overhead projection system incorporates a tilted wall screen as well as a tilted projection stand—both of which can be adjusted by the teacher.

Obviously, if the projector is used at your normal standing or sitting level, many students' line of sight can be blocked by the projector and the teacher. Careful placement of students, projector, and screen avoid this problem.

Auxiliary Equipment. The overhead itself should be a sufficient boon to teachers. However, some ingenious devices have been developed

to make the projector even more valuable. Each will be coverved specifically in application sections later in this chapter. They are: the
overhead science projector (or attachment), the polarizer, transparent
film roll, tachistoscope, and rear projection screen. Not all projectors
can be equipped with all these special features, so check carefully for
any desired feature before you buy.

The Transparency. Transparencies used for overhead projection
are generally sheets of clear or matte acetate mounted in heavy tagboard
frames. Images are impressed on the acetate by a variety of chemical
or mechanical processes which are explained in succeeding pages.

Transparency sizes most frequently found are 5″ x 5″, 7″ x 7″, and
8″ x 10″, with 8″ x 10″ the most widespread. Transparencies are often
found without mounting frames—the acetate base serves instead.

Making and Using Transparencies

In the early 1960's, a standard college audiovisual textbook observed that there were very few commercially produced educational
transparencies available. Just a few years later, thousands were on the
market.

But part of the contention still holds true. Many teachers still want
to use transparencies which simply do not exist. The answer—do it yourself!

HANDMADE SLIDES

The easiest transparency to make is the handmade type. Many
techniques can be used; a variety of media can be employed.

Freehand. Writing and drawing on clear acetate may be done with
an ordinary "grease" or "china marking" pencil. Projected grease pencil
images always appear "black" on the screen since the thick crayonlike
writing substance is opaque and blocks passage of light to the screen.
All grease pencil drawn transparencies, therefore, appear only in black
and white. Grease pencils are hard to point, and become dull very
easily. Marks made on acetate may be removed by rubbing them with a
dry cloth or tissue. The slide can be completely cleaned by soaking the
cloth with any standard non-flammable cleaning fluid (such as per-
chlorethelene).

Color makes a transparency come to life, and you'll need to know a
few of the many ways it can be accomplished!

Pencils. When you're working on a matte surface slide, water
soluble pencils may be used to color a pencil or ink drawing you've made

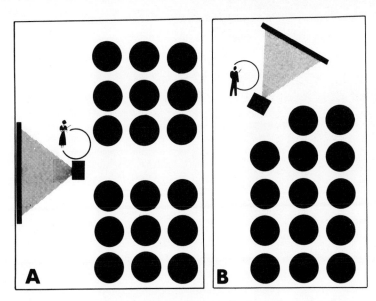

Fig. 3.5—In order to achieve better viewing of overhead projection transparencies, seating is often arranged as shown here. Figure A indicates the "empty aisle" system, and Figure B depicts the "oblique" placement method. Both types can provide full viewing for all students.

Fig. 3.6—The unmounted transparency is made entirely of one sheet of plastic. Some, as the one shown, are fairly rigid and may successfully be used without mounting. Thinner unmounted transparencies should be placed in readymade cardboard mounts, as the one shown in Figure 3.8.

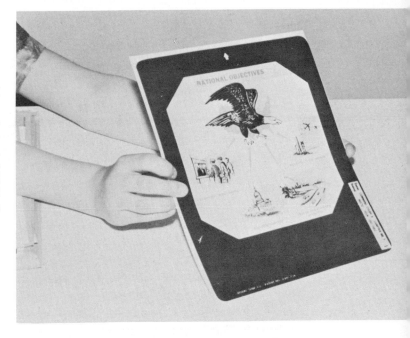

on the slide. After coloring you can moisten the colored area with a fine brush. The brush should be almost dry or the soluble color could streak excessively. Some pencil users prefer to omit the brushing step. Regardless which method you prefer, the color should be sealed in with

Fig. 3.7—Where fine hand lettering or drawing is needed, transparent colors may be applied with fine line plastic tip flow pens, as the Pentel® in use here.

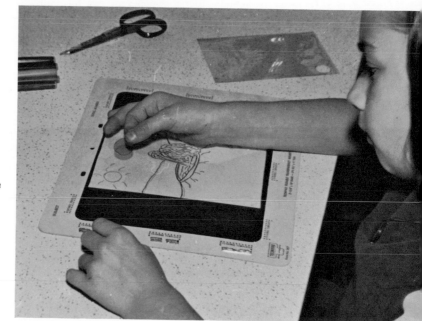

Fig. 3.8—Applying Adhesive Color Film

a clear plastic aerosol spray. The spray will brighten color somewhat, and will change uncolored areas, when projected, from gray to white.

Coloring on clear acetate can be done easily, too, with a special translucent slide pencil sold by all audiovisual supply houses.

Liquid Inks. Inks are made in two types, permanent solvent base acetate inks, and water base inks. They may be applied by drawing pen, brush, or airbrush.

48

The water base inks have a special wetting agent additive which lets them flow on acetate. Ordinary water ink merely forms droplets on the acetate surface, so it is of little value for transparency coloring.

Solvent type inks are generally dissolved colored acetate dyes. They provide a much deeper color than pencils, but they are more difficult to use.

At best, inks give uneven coloration when applied by brush or lettering pen. Airbrush techniques do a much finer job, but substantial practice is needed to become proficient at airbrushing.

Whenever water base inks are used, a clear plastic spray should be used to "fix" the colors.

Flow Pens. Felt and plastic fiber tip pens can be used as a coloring medium too. Solid, even color cannot be achieved; rather, an artistic streaked color effect results. Early flow pens, such as the Magic Marker® or Flo-Master®, gave broad, bold streaks of color, but were not at all satisfactory for fine lettering or detail work. The plastic fiber tip, a later development by the Japanese Pentel Pen Company, writes in 8 colors and can form lines as narrow as $\frac{1}{32}$ of an inch. The water base ink adheres well to acetate, and it can be removed with a damp cloth if you make a mistake. Similar pens are now available from many manufacturers.

Color Film. One of the best ways to achieve even color on a hand made transparency is with colored plastic film. The type made especially for this use is coated with a pressure sensitive adhesive and backed by a release paper or film. In selecting adhesive color film, try to obtain one which has a transparent backing sheet. Your color application process will be greatly simplified. Here's how it's done:

1. Place a film of the desired color over the transparency area to be colored.
2. Trace the outline of the area onto the film with a china marking pencil.
3. Cut the color film (and its release backing) to the desired shape.
4. Peel the release, and apply the color film to the proper area of the transparency.

Dry Color. This recent development allows you to deposit a solid sheet of color *only*—exactly where you want it, without the buildup of layers of acetate which you have with adhesive color film. All you do is burnish down the dry color and peel away the carrying film. Only a pure color layer is left on the transparency. Since the dye layers are transparent, one color may be superimposed upon another to obtain still a third color. Dry color is also available in pattern sheets.

Lettering the Transparency. The techniques described here are not necessarily limited to the handmade transparency, where you're working directly on the final slide. Many of them may be used in making "masters" to be used later in various photographic, thermal or chemical slide making processes, which are explained in this chapter.

Size. The first consideration in transparency lettering is size. A great many "rules" can be found for determining minimum letter height and weight (line thickness), and some are so complicated as to require an engineering or mathematics degree just to understand them. You'll probably make letters of the "right" size if you consider this: Minimum letter size must be determined by the maximum distance at which the projected image will be viewed, and the overall size of the projected image.

For example, if a projected 8″ x 10″ transparency fills a 40″ x 40″ screen, and is viewed from a distance of 25 feet, ¼″ letter height is adequate. But with the same screen conditions, and a viewing distance of 75 feet, the minimum letter height for readability is *over* ½ *inch.* Since most teacher prepared transparencies will be used in classrooms (approximately 35′ long) on about a 50 x 50 inch screen, a ¾₁₆″ letter would be the minimum size.

Fig. 3.9–(*3 M Company*)

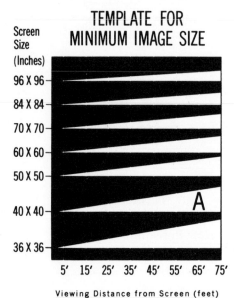

TEMPLATE FOR MINIMUM IMAGE SIZE

Screen Size (Inches)

Viewing Distance from Screen (feet)

Determine the screen size and the maximum viewing distance—Place this template over the original to determine the minimum image size as illustrated by the letter **A** above

Fig. 3.10–Press letters used on transparencies may be opaque or of transparent color. The letters on the left (AAA) are transparent, as shown by the fact that three opaque lines drawn on the blank transparency may be seen *through* the AAA. They will project in color. The letters on the right (XYZ), are opaque, and they will project in black, regardless what the color of the letters may be.

Press Letters. The easiest method of hand lettering, and one that gives the most professional results—is the use of press-on letters. These letters are printed on a carrier sheet and then transferred to transparency or artwork by burnishing the carrier sheet over the desired letter. The adhesive used leaves no visible residue during projection. Since the carrier sheet is transparent, proper letter positioning is a simple matter. As is true with dry transfer color, press on letters are available in transparent colors [1]; projected letters will appear in color. Any opaque letter will appear black on the screen.

Press letters have one major disadvantage. They will not withstand severe handling or any abrasion. After the transparency has been lettered with press letters, a sheet of clear acetate should be permanently affixed as a protective layer.

Lettering Guides and Templates. These devices are an important aid to lettering, but not all can be used in lettering directly on the transparency. Even with special pens and inks, there is a tendency for acetate ink to "creep." It is extremely important that the guide be raised sufficiently above the acetate to prevent the ink from creeping under the guide. To accomplish this, the guide is usually undercut. If it is not, you'll have to provide some means of raising it about $\frac{1}{16}''$ to $\frac{1}{8}''$ above the acetate. Special pens (such as the Koh-i-noor Acetograph®, can be used with most lettering guides and are able to carry solvent base acetate inks.

Template devices (Leroy®, Letterguide®, etc.) are difficult to use on acetate, but they are capable of providing quality lettering on any paper surface. You can become quite proficient in the use of template type lettering tools, but a great deal of practice is needed.

Films and Carbons. Special "carbon" papers can be used for typing directly onto acetate. Pica type can be used for transparencies to be used in normal size classrooms. Elite type will be too small. If you have an oversize face typewriter (e.g. Primary Manuscript), it will be ideal for this use.

In use, the acetate transparency and the carbon are sandwiched together. Typing is done directly onto the carbon paper. The projected result is a black caption on a white background.

Vu-Graph Film® may be used to create white lettering against a black background. Sandwich the film together with a sheet of 9 lb. typing paper (onion skin), and insert it into the typewriter so that

---

[1] Transparent press-on letters are available under such trade names as Color-Stik, Deka-Dry, Project-a-type, Graf-type, Instant Lettering.

typing will be done on the tissue. Carbon will offset from the film to the paper, leaving the film clear where the type impression was received.

Airbrushing. Using an airbrush on a transparency is decidedly not one of the easier techniques. But if you want to try your hand at a different medium which allows you to achieve color gradation (from light to dark or *vice versa*), airbrushing is for you.

While there are two commonly used types of airbrush, the double action and the single action, only the single action will be treated here. The double action is an expensive professional graphic arts tool which would hardly be available to the teacher.

In the single action airbrush both color and "air" are released simultaneously with a push of the button. A portable airbrush unit with an independent compressed gas (air) supply can be inexpensively purchased for use with some airbrushes.

"Air" is supplied to the brush from the source via a small hose. The flow of air through the brush and out the nozzle draws with it a small quantity of paint (ink). This quantity can be adjusted at the nozzle. The flow of gas is controlled by a valve on the can of freon gas.

The freon gas is stored in the can as a liquid. As gas is drawn off through airbrushing, the can begins to freeze and the working pressure drops. When this occurs, stop working, shut off the gas supply, and allow the can to assume room temperature. Naturally the gas should not be allowed to flow unless you are actually airbrushing.

Solvent base inks which will adhere to acetate must be used, such as Speedry Type A®, Keystone Lantern Slide Inks® and Paasche Weather Resistant Colors®.

If you're new to airbrushing, or if you haven't tried it in some time, don't get right to work on a transparency. Practice first on some scrap material. To get approximate effect of the way the color will appear when projected, work over a light box.

While texts on airbrushing techniques are available for persons in the graphic arts, the basic elements which the transparency maker needs to know are contained in this excerpt: [2]

> Free brush exercises can be practiced within "A" and "B," two parallel lines six inches apart on a sheet of drawing paper. Airbrush motion should begin approximately one inch to the left of line "A," and continue in a smooth stroking motion to the right, beyond line "B." The control valve is depressed immediately before reaching line "A," and held down until line "B" is crossed.

---

[2] "Airbrushing ABECDARY," *Visucom*, Vol. 1, No. 4 (1961), pp. 11-14.

Fig. 3.11—Inexpensive, portable airbrushes, such as the Wren® use canned Freon gas as the "air" source. A finger controlled button releases both paint and "air" for use.

Fig. 3.12—Airbrushing is not difficult, but practice is needed to master the techniques described in the text.

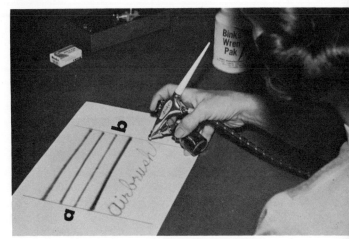

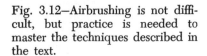

The airbrush is operated by "strokes" in a steady right-to-left, or left-to-right motion; at the same distance above the work, throughout the stroke. Strokes must continue evenly to at least an inch beyond the area to be colored. On the return stroke, the reverse order should be followed. The stroke begins an inch beyond line "B"; the valve is depressed immediately before arriving at "B"; color is applied from "B" to "A"; the valve is released at "A," and the stroke is continued smoothly beyond "A."

Before using pigments, practice elementary stroking to obtain "sound" and "feel" of the brush. When a free, smooth arm movement has been acquired, fill the color-bottle with ink, and practice applying the color.

Experiment by holding the brush at varying distances from the paper, and notice the different widths of area covered. Note what occurs when the brush is held too close to the paper and without a "Follow-through" when it is stopped at the end of the stroke. Also, experiment moving the brush at varying speeds with different spray adjustments.

Practice exercises will accustom you to the weight, feel, and motion of the brush. Once this technique has been mastered, beautiful, and soft-blended color effects can be obtained; particularly on projectuals with negative, or dark, backgrounds.

"Free-brush" requires no masking, or "frisketing." The airbrush is adjusted for width of spray, and worked as closely as possible within the subject outline. Overspray should not cause concern. It may actually be used to good advantage. The overspray of several colors will create soft blendings between different areas. Free-brush is excellent for suggesting backgrounds, sky, fur, cloth and skin tones.

Masking and Frisketing

Sharp edges are needed to differentiate color in buildings, boxes, bar graphs, etc. These edges are obtained by a "frisket," or mask which covers one area while another area is being airbrushed. Frisket paper is thin and semitransparent. It may be purchased either prepared or unprepared. Prepared frisket has an adhesive applied to one side. Unprepared frisket paper must be coated on one side with thinned rubber cement. When the cement is dry, a second coat should be applied. This produces a tacky surface, which is applied directly to the artwork. The artwork to be airbrushed is outlined with a sharp knife or razor blade, care being taken not to cut the surface of the projectual. The frisket is stripped away from the area to be airbrushed.

Masks perform the same function. They are not cemented to the artwork, but are held in place with small weights. Masks can be prepared from clear acetate, card stock, or heavy paper.

Diazo Transparencies

Diazo chemistry is complex, but transparency making with diazo film is quite easy.

Clear acetate is coated with a diazo salt, a "coupler," and a mild acid. The diazo is usually a pale yellow, and it is this that gives unexposed diazo film its characteristic color.

In the acid environment of the sensitized coating, the color coupler and diazo salt do not react. However, in an alkaline ammonia environment, the sensitized layer on the film would rapidly become a solid color (according to the color forming properties of the particular diazo salt used).

The characteristic of the sensitized layer which lets us make transparencies is the fact that the diazo salt converts to a new compound, unable to form color, when the sensitized layer is exposed to ultraviolet light. Incandescent room light and diffused sunlight ordinarily do not contain enough UV to "burn out" the sensitized layer, so diazo transparencies need not be made in darkness.

It follows then, that any area of the diazo sensitized film which is covered by a material opaque to ultraviolet light will, after development, appear as a solid color.

The converse is also true and important in diazo transparency making. That is, any material which does *not* block UV light will *permit* the conversion of diazo salts in any area it covers.

Diazo reproduction is direct, that is, the copy is the same size as the original. It is also positive, since a positive original produces a positive copy.

Making a Master. A diazo master must be made on a translucent or transparent base. The best such material is specially prepared translucent diazo paper, but ordinary onion skin will serve in an emergency. The master is prepared, as original artwork, by any normal drawing techniques which employ opaque line. This can be accomplished with ease since the translucent master base is paper, not acetate as the hand-made transparency is. Any lettering, drawing, or diagram from other sources may just be traced onto the master, for the master base is thin enough to permit easy "see through."

But suppose you want to use printed artwork or lettering from books, magazines and newspapers. This can be done too, by any of four methods:

1. Photographic. The subject matter can be photographed and a positive transparency made from the negative. When this method is used, enlargement or reduction is possible.

2. Autopositive. Certain translucent base photographic papers can be used to make a diazo reproducible print. Autopositive paper is developed in ordinary photo paper developer, but in subdued room light, not in darkness or under a safelight. (See page 63 for autopositive technique.)

3. Reflex. A translucent copy can be made using any number of reflex photocopy machines. (Sears 3M, Apeco, Contura-Constat®, etc.)

4. Electrostatic. A "Xerox"® copy can be made on translucent paper. Some Xerox service organizations are equipped to enlarge or reduce the image too.

It must be remembered that most diazo films reproduce only *one* color. Therefore, all opaque images on the translucent master will appear in the same color. If you want your transparency to appear in multiple colors, you'll need a separate master and film for each color. The individual diazo transparencies, after development, are then mounted together in proper registry to form one colored slide.

Just as pre-printed tapes, patterns, and letters were used in making handmade slides, they can be used in diazo master preparation too. However, colored or transparent materials cannot be used since the printed parts must be opaque to ultra-violet light, and some colors pass it in varying degrees. Only black or special dense brown images block UV effectively enough for use on diazo masters.

The selection of pre-printed materials grows larger each day! In addition to the samples shown in Figure 3.13, you can have patterns showing engraving screens, cross-hatch, stippling, dashes, brick patterns —and countless others. Pre-printed diazo patterns and tapes have a special adhesive which is not sensitive to heat, for incandescent printing lamps radiate a great deal of heat.

Printing a Diazo Master. Large, costly machines are available for printing diazo sensitized materials. But they aren't a "must." This is not to say that the well equipped school instructional materials center won't have a diazo printer. On the contrary, it will. But if you don't have one in your school, you can make high quality transparencies with an ordinary wooden photographic printing frame, a large "pickle" jar, and a bit of commercial Aqua Ammonia. You'll need a sunny day, too.

Loading the Frame. First, choose the right diazo film for the final color you desire. All film packages are clearly labeled. For best results, place the face of the master (the side on which you've been working) in contact with the sensitized side of the diazo film. You can tell which is the sensitized side by either referring to the manufacturer's instruction sheet which accompanies each package—or by the "old time" method— touching the tip of your tongue to a corner of each side. The sensitized side will give a slight taste of the diazo salt.

Place the master-film sandwich in the printing frame with the back side of the master visible through the glass of the printing frame—then lock the frame lid securely in place. All of this can be done in normal or subdued incandescent room light.

Printing. Now we come to the sunny day requirement. Since sunlight is an excellent source of UV light, it can be used for diazo printing. However, unlike the controlled light source of the commercial printer, you'll have to experiment to determine correct exposure time. One thing is certain. You won't get uniform results if the sun is peeking in and out of clouds. The condition should be constant and even sunlight.

A test exposure can be made by exposing a film through a translucent master on which you've drawn an india ink line from end to end. The test exposure is made by loading the frame as before, and exposing parts of the test strip progressively, 30 seconds at a time. If you have 10 sections, each representing a 30 second exposure, the developed test

Fig. 3.13—A wide variety of tape is available for use on transparencies. Pre-printed tapes are particularly useful in making technical charts and graph transparencies. (*Materials courtesy of Chart-Pak, Inc.*)

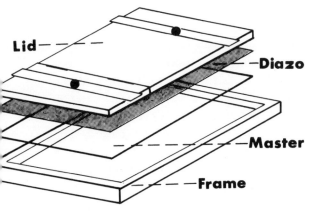

Fig. 3.14—Blowup of the frame and materials used in diazo printing.

Fig. 3.15—Since diazo materials are sensitive to ultra-violet light, printing of a diazo transparency can be done in sunlight, which is rich in U-V.

strip will show you the color obtained for exposures of 30 seconds, 1 minute, 1½ minutes, and so forth. Again, because it is so very important, the sunlight must be of constant value.

Once you've determined the proper exposure, you're ready to print and develop your master.

If you want to try diazo work with the printing frame, but you find that sunlight is too erratic, satisfactory results can be obtained by using reflector photoflood lamps in a bank of 4. Here too, exposure tests will have to be made to determine correct printing time.

Fig. 3.16—Development of a diazo transparency is done in a room normally lighted with incandescent lamps by merely inserting the exposed foil into a pickle jar containing ammonia fumes. (*A. Winegarden*)

Development of a Diazo. The pickle jar method of diazo development is certainly not the most rapid, but it is the best for the beginner—for he can see the film developing.

To develop a diazo, you must first prepare the development container. It must be air tight and capable of being rapidly closed. The reason is simple. Ammonia is the diazo developer, and the fumes, if excessive, can be annoying. The room in which development is done should be ventilated. The container itself is activated by placing a cellulose sponge in the bottom of the jar and pouring 2 or 3 ounces of Aqua Ammonia over it. Then seal the jar.

To develop a diazo, merely roll up the film, lift the jar lid, and insert the rolled film inside. Then rapidly close the jar again.[3]

Development normally takes from 2 to 4 minutes, and the process is visible through the pickle jar.

Overlays. If overlays are desired, additional masters will be needed, and each one must be printed on a diazo film of the desired color potential. When mounted, each must be carefully placed in proper registry.

Multiple Color Development. Generally a diazo film contains only one color. There are exceptions which you might want to try.

If you have simple line drawings with several colors, and sequential presentation is *not* needed, there are films which permit you to develop as many as 5 colors on one film. (Varicolor, Copyflex, etc.) The methods used to achieve multi-color effects vary slightly in the films of different manufacturers.

Basically, however, you have to paint certain areas with different color forming solutions. The method is not practical when colored areas come adjacent to each other.

---

[3] A special jar and cover unit is marketed by the Tecnifax Corporation. It enables you to press a lever to open the jar; releasing, it snaps the cover tightly closed. The rapid action lessens ammonia fumes which escape into the room.

Another interesting material is the two color diazo film. Each side is sensitized with a different diazo salt and the center acetate base is made to block ultra-violet light. In practice, this system gives 3 colors, for where the developed images on both sides *overlap,* a third color is created.

For exposure, film of this type is generally placed between *two* masters, and each side of the film successively exposed. Development is by the standard ammonia vapor method.

It is interesting to note that only two sheets of film can give you all colors of the spectrum. Since one set of primary light colors is composed of yellow, cyan and magenta, a cyan-magenta double film, and a yellow single diazo can, when projected in a properly overlapping manner, produce all spectral colors.

Mounting Transparencies. Transparency mounts should be purchased from dealers and used for all transparencies. Even if only a single sheet is used, the mount serves as a protection. If overlays are used, they can be hinged to the mount, thus removing the possibility of damage to the transparency. (Note: A few commercial transparencies use very thick acetate sheets as a base and the base itself is designed to be the mount.)

Pre-Printed Masters. For those teachers who want to make transparencies, but would rather not make the masters, many diazo film manufacturers sell such masters inexpensively (or even give them away) so that the teacher will use the diazo process. Since availability of pre-printed translucent masters changes rapidly, it is best to write to manufacturers to determine *current* policy.

Fig. 3.17—Some commercial concerns print inexpensive masters which enable the user to make his own transparencies. In this one, by printing masters on foils of different color forming qualities, a full color transparency may be made. (*Tecnifax Corporation*)

Fig. 3.18—The easiest transparency to make, next to the handmade, is the thermal type. Master and sensitized plastic sheet are inserted into the copier, and, 4 seconds later, a usable transparency appears! (*A. Winegarden*)

Thermal Transparencies [4]

Where the diazo transparency was UV sensitive, the thermal transparency is heat (infra red) sensitive. It, too, is a direct, not a negative, process.

The thermal process is certainly the quickest and easiest to use *if* your thermal copy machine is clean and *if* you have made test exposures. There is little that can match the dramatic effect of showing your class a map clipping from the morning newspaper, and projecting a transparency of it on a screen less than 10 seconds later!

Another major advantage of the thermal method is that it is completely dry. Thus you can make transparencies without any messy chemical mixing or pouring and without decrease in solution strength due to periods of disuse. And for schools where there isn't constant use, this is an important advantage over liquid chemical methods.

The basic problem is that there is no inexpensive way to start. The use of the thermal method *requires* a thermal copy machine. Numerous attempts by the author to develop a do-it-yourself non-machine method of making thermal transparencies all resulted in failure.

But, if your school office already uses a thermal copier, an "O.K." from the principal and a few sheets of transparency film are all you'll need to get started making instant (4 second) transparencies.

Making a thermal transparency is easiest of all—if you take into account certain limitations which never seem to be mentioned. It will not copy all colors (in black and white, of course); nor will it reproduce a color illustration adequately in black and white. But it is ideal for producing quick transparencies of black printed line originals, typewritten copy, or pencil written matter. Special thermographic ball-points must be used if ball-point pen writing is to be reproduced.

---

[4] See also Morton J. Shultz, "Teacher and Overhead Projection" (Englewood Cliffs, N.J.: Prentice-Hall, Inc., 1965).

But the process is so simple, you should try it. The original and the copy film are placed in contact with each other, the machine is set for the appropriate density level, and the film and master are inserted. Four seconds later the sandwich has passed through the machine and the transparency is made! With some films a special carrier must be used. The film and master are placed in this carrier before development in the copier.

Color film is made in two varieties. In one type the image appears colored on a black background; in the other, the image appears black on a color tint background. The range of colors is very limited when compared to diazo films available.

Color lift transparencies can be made on the thermal copier with a special laminating film, but this can be done just as easily without a machine as explained on page 15.

Fig. 3.19—This versatile copy unit makes a transparency from any color original in about 1 minute. First, the carrying case which also doubles as the exposure unit is lifted from the base which serves as the developer unit (top left). Then the original and an intermediate sheet are placed beneath a glass plate which is contained in a compartment in the base. The exposure unit is fitted over the plate (top right) and original and intermediate are exposed to light for several seconds. Next, the intermediate and a sheet of transparency film or copy paper are placed together in the developer unit (lower left). After a few seconds the image forms. The operator can check it visually to see when it has reached the proper stage of development (lower right), and he can stop the process when satisfactory development is reached. (3 M Company)

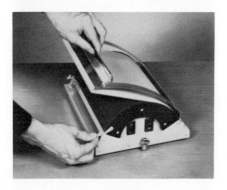

Another thermal device which is especially interesting for the school, due to its low cost, is the two step transparency maker-copier. In this completely dry process the exposure unit and an intermediate "negative" are placed over the original to be copied. The unit can copy from books, or even from a wall chart. After about a 30 second exposure, the "negative" intermediate is placed on a second unit together with a sheet of transparency film, and developed. Thermal development is completed in another 30 seconds. However, in this system, like the diazo, you can see the image developing so you can remove it at any time— before or after the normal development period.

Thermal Spirit Duplicator Transparency Masters. Many thermal copy machines are able to make spirit duplicator masters of any subject which can be thermo-copied. The masters are suitable for short class-room size runs. Spirit masters are made by placing the material to be copied and the thermal spirit master set into a copy sleeve and then into the copier. The resulting master can be used to run up to 100 copies. Then, as an added bonus, you spray the dye carrying master with a transparent plastic, and it becomes a projection transparency. Your students can follow your class instruction when you use the transparency, and can later do an individual assignment with their own copies.

Photographic Transparencies

There are tens of ways to produce photographic transparencies. They all have two similarities: Exposure is by light and development is chemical. Most have an intermediate negative stage, and some are direct positives.

Photographic copying, in its many variations, has the advantage of being able to "see" most colors and convert them to black and white (blue usually does not copy well).

Fine detail can be reproduced by photographic means, too.

The master for a photographic transparency may be prepared on any white paper by any standard writing, drawing, printing or paste up method.

Methods of Preparation. There are three methods of photo transparency preparation which are practical for the teacher.

The first is practical only when the finest detail is needed, and when the teacher using it is something of a camera buff. A photographic film negative from any standard camera is enlarged onto a sheet of 8 x 10 photographic film, which is then developed in a high contrast developer. The positive print which results, since it is on a transparent base, is ideal for an overhead slide. The limiting factor in this method is the degree of darkroom proficiency you'll need and the cost of materials. But it does have the advantage of being able to make an 8 x 10 transparency out of any size original, regardless how large or small. Color transparencies can be made in this size, too, but this task is not suited to local production —and the cost is phenomenal!

The second photographic method uses a Verifax® type office copy machine and Verifax Transparent Sheeting®. This method produces the best detail possible in non-camera methods when used in conjunction with a FineLine Matrix®. Any original may be copied—whether typed, drawn, printed in crayon, pencil, ink, etc. However, the ability to produce fine detail, while a tremendous advantage, can operate to your detriment. Remember that there are minimum sizes in letter and detail— and to go below the minimum reduces the useful viewing distance of the transparency tremendously.

This method is just as easy as making an ordinary office paper copy, but instead of loading the copier with copy paper, use Kodak Transparent Sheeting #1632®.

Place the sheeting in the copier paper compartment with the matte side of the sheeting down (Emulsion side is glossy).

Expose a Verifax® matrix master (any colors, any medium) for about 90% of normal exposure. The matrix is then chemically activated by whatever method your particular model Verifax® uses. Then withdraw the matrix in contact with the sheeting and strip them apart rapidly. Your transparency will have black letters on a matte white background. For best results allow it to dry a few minutes before use.

A third photographic method which requires no special equipment is the autopositive process. The emulsion of autopositive paper and film reacts slowly to light, so it can be processed and developed under normal room illumination.

To make an autopositive transparency you will need Autopositive Transparency Film®, Sheeting Yellow® (an ultra violet), a photo paper developer setup (Dektol®, stopbath and Fixer), a printing frame, and a strong incandescent light source (4 reflector photo floods).

Sheeting Yellow® is placed next to the glass of the printing frame. Next, the autopositive film is placed in the frame with the emulsion side facing up (away from the Sheeting Yellow®). Then your original (master) to be copied is placed in the frame so that the material to be copied contacts the emulsion side of the film. Firm contact is extremely important.

When printing autopositive film under these conditions, you should make a test exposure strip by varying the exposure to light in the same manner as with diazo film. If exposure was too short, the white areas will not be clear; if exposure was too long, the white areas will be clear, but parts of the image will appear faded or obliterated.

As an alternate exposure light source, some AV specialists recommend using the stage of the overhead projector.

Autopositive development is accomplished by immersing the film in a standard paper developer (such as Dektol®). When the image fully appears, transfer the film to an acid stop bath, and after about 20 seconds, to a photographic fixer solution. The transparency should remain in the fixer for 10 to 15 minutes. When the film is removed from the fixer, it should be washed well in running water and air dried.

For information purposes only, you should know that there are other methods of transparency production. Mass produced slides are often printed with transparent inks. Electrostatic printing on acetate can deposit an opaque image, reduced, enlarged or the same size as the original (master).

Special Effects, Techniques and Equipment

Using the Overlay. Whenever you need to present information sequentially, the transparency overlay is an ideal tool.

In basic sequence presentation, you make a separate transparency for each component of information. Two methods of overlay attachment are used. In the first an overlay is placed in registry over the static slide, and hinged at one edge in book page fashion. Succeeding overlays are attached in similar manner.

Of course, overlays attached along one edge of the static can only be used in the same order during each presentation. It follows that only some types of sequential presentation are suited to this binding—subjects which will always be presented in the same order.

For example, a transparency showing territorial expansion of the United States by means of overlays could easily be hinged on one edge since there wouldn't be any reason to present acquisitions in any order other than chronological.

But, if the transparency overlays are designed to present variations on the static slide, they must be hinged to both side, top and bottom of the mount. This type of presentation requires the static to be shown continuously and the overlays to be used alternately.

Such an overlay system is valuable in many subjects.

Fig. 3.20—The flipover system may be used to present information sequentially. The number of overlays which can be used is theoretically unlimited, as long as they are attached in proper sequence. Practically, however, reduction in light output and mechanical considerations limits the number of overlays to 5 or 6 (maximum). (*Tecnifax Corporation*)

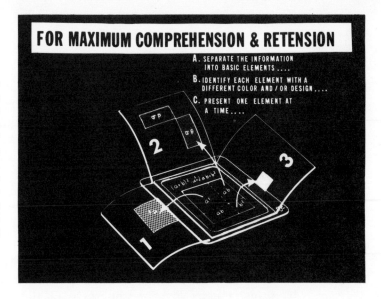

FOR MAXIMUM COMPREHENSION & RETENSION

A. SEPARATE THE INFORMATION INTO BASIC ELEMENTS....

B. IDENTIFY EACH ELEMENT WITH A DIFFERENT COLOR AND / OR DESIGN....

C. PRESENT ONE ELEMENT AT A TIME....

Overlay Testing. Some visuals lend themselves not only to instruction, but also to evaluation.

If you use a transparency to show the parts of a flower, you can use that same slide to test what knowledge has been gained.

Place a sheet of clear acetate over the last overlay. Mount the acetate with overlay hinges, or with a piece of pressure sensitive tape. Then block out the names of the parts to be identified with segments of opaque tape. Using press-on letters, label each block A, B, C, D, etc. A quick quiz then becomes a simple matter, for after instruction on flower parts, simply flip your last overlay and the test is on the screen. This technique can be used with any subject matter which uses short answers.

Still and Animated Objects. Since the projector stage is horizontal, a great deal can be accomplished with it.

If the physical education instructor makes a grid of a football or baseball field on a static transparency, solid objects can be used to show proper moves of players for various plays. Any small objects will do, but team members should be identified by using objects of different shape.

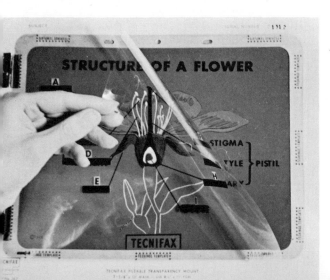

Fig. 3.21—Opaque tape properly placed on an overlay and identified by letters or numbers, turns a transparency into a testing device.

Different colors can be used if you secure pieces of transparent plastic (primary grade counting discs are fine). The same technique can be used in any situation which requires movement of objects—such as car and pedestrian movement in a safety or driver training class; movement of ships on a static may be used to show exploration; relative movement of sun and planets or earth and moon, and movement of atoms in chemical equations for your own subject areas.

Standard materials such as transparent plastic rulers, protractors, templates, etc. can be easily projected. Some special devices are made just for overhead projection too—slide rulers, clock faces, meshing gears, electric meters, and basic physics mechanisms.

Fluids. Certain chemical and physical reactions may be observed by using a petri dish on the stage of the projector. This method is especially effective when there's a color change involved in the reaction.

Surface tension can be shown by placing a few drops of water in the petri dish, and then adding a few drops of a surface tension reducer, as Kodak Photo-Flo®, or any liquid household detergent.

Graphic Charts. Transparencies made from standard forms or charts let the instructor point out visually what he is discussing. Secondary teachers can use this system for bookkeeping and Internal Revenue forms. It is also suited to making slides of attendance record forms, official school registers, cumulative records, and other forms studied at teacher staff meetings.

Tachistoscopic Projection. Some OHPs can be equipped with a special attachment which can aid in remedial reading and identification of objects. This device is merely a timer which is attached to the lens and allows light to pass through for only a brief period. Thus words, sentences, or pictures can be flashed on the screen to encourage rapid identification.

Polarizing materials placed on the transparency cause a motion effect when subjected to varying polarization obtained by rotating a polarizing filter in the light beam of the overhead projector.

Fig. 3.22A   Fig. 3.22B

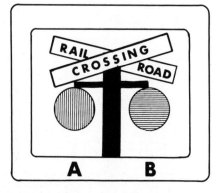
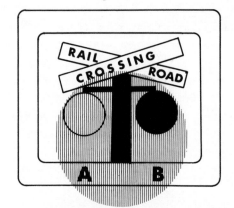

Polarized Projection. In recent years, light polarizing filters have been used on the transparency and on the lens to achieve rather startling results on the screen—"blinking" lights, various types of motion, and spectacular kaleidoscope color.

The blinking effect is best demonstrated with a transparency of a railroad crossing signal. The light coming through the circles "A" and "B" of Figure 1 is polarized by the filter material placed over each circle, with the polarization stress lines in the positions shown.

It can then be readily seen that another polarization filter which is positioned over the transparency (Fig. 2) will pass the light of flasher "A" to the screen and cancel out the light of flasher "B." As this super-imposed filter is rotated, the lines of polarization will align with those of "B," and "A" will be cancelled out. The effect on the screen is that of a railroad crossing blinker in action.

The second major polarization effect is motion. Commercially pre-pared sheets of cellophane-like birefringent materials are available, which, when properly applied to transparencies will produce the illusion of flow, turbulence, reversing, blinking, and rotary action. Since the commercially prepared material incorporates one of the necessary polar-ization filters within it, the only filter necessary for use is attached to the lens of the projector.

Science Projection. Science teachers can be aided by a special overhead projector, the Act-O-Matic®, which is designed for the specific purpose of projecting test tube reactions. In addition, there are special attachments which fit *certain* projectors and allow test tube projection.

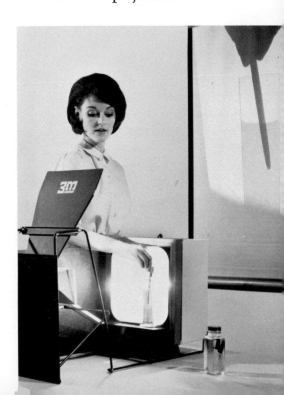

Fig. 3.23—The overhead projector can be placed on its side and used with an attachment to show test tube demonstrations greatly en-larged. (*3 M Company*)

Fig. 3.24—The "moving chalkboard" is created by using a roll of acetate as a writing surface instead of a transparency. A mere turn of a knob returns anything written into instant view. (*A. Winegarden*)

With most such units, the projector must be turned on its side. This is not as formidable a problem as it appears, since projectors which have science attachments available are all of the lightweight type.

Roll Attachment. If you want to use the overhead as a lighted chalkboard, try the cellophane roll attachment. You can write to your heart's content, and then—instead of erasing—just turn a crank, and *voilà*, a clean area of cellophane awaits your pen! Anything that can be written on a chalkboard can be written on an overhead roll. But the overhead has advantages over a chalkboard:

1. Since it's lighted, the OH screen acts as an attention getter.

2. You can "erase" by turning the roll, but unlike the chalkboard, you can make your writing re-appear by merely turning it back.

3. You show only what you want to. If you have to write large quantities of material on your chalkboard, good teaching practice dictates that only the material actually being used should be visible to students. With a standard chalkboard—this means that your whole room would have draped chalkboards! But with an acetate roll on an overhead —just turn the crank!

Teaching Tips. With a machine as versatile as the overhead, you've probably developed ideas of your own about use techniques and subject matter, but, if you haven't, here are a few to start you off:

• *Placing the Transparency on the Stage* seems like child's play— but there's a right way and a wrong way. As a teacher, you must be concerned with getting full impact from the materials you use. That impact can be lost if you turn on the light switch and then place and center the transparency on the stage. This step should be performed with the projection lamp *off.* Don't let your class see you doing the preliminary work. Rather, show the transparency exactly when needed.

• *Hold the Static* transparency firmly when flipping overlays. The flipping can cause the transparency to move distractingly across the stage.

• *Experiment with Unusual Materials* such as coins, fabrics, leaves, and other opaque patterned materials. It isn't necessary to use transparencies all the time.

• *Try Using Part of a Transparency.* Revelation, or progressive disclosure technique is quite effective. A transparency which has *multiple* parts which you'd like to present individually is merely covered with an opaque sheet (black construction paper will do). Just slide the paper away at will, revealing only what you want to show. The same effect can be achieved by cutting out little windows and covering them. When each cover is lifted, the image in that window is projected.

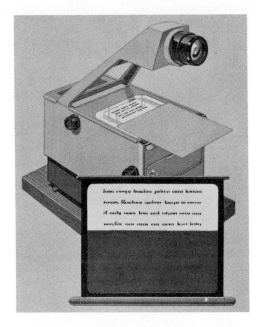

Fig. 3.25—Try attracting attention by revealing your message to students only a bit at a time. It prevents distraction by forcing students to concentrate only on the desired part which is being projected. (*3 M Company*)

• *The Lightboard®* is an ingenious use of the old principle—the magic slate. Place the Lightboard® on the stage and write on it with a stylus. White writing will appear on a dark background.

• *You Don't Need a Screen* for all types of transparency projection. The OHP can be effectively used on a chalkboard or a flannel board due to its high light intensity. When used with the flannelboard, the overhead not only places a basic diagram on it, but also serves to illuminate any objects on the board.

• *Map Making* with the overhead is a simple matter. Using a transparency as the basic map, you can trace the map outline on the chalkboard directly and accurately. Actually, any line drawing can be transferred in this manner.

• *Student Sentence Structure Can be "Critiqued"* easily if pupils are given lined acetate to work on. The finished lesson can then be placed on the projector stage and discussed by the teacher and class. Specific points can be indicated in color using fine line marking pens.

If work is done on 9 lb. paper and treated with a transparentizer solution, you will still be able to project, though the room will have to be in darkness.

This critique technique may be used for any subject, and is particularly useful in language, handwriting, mathematics and science—where the written or drawn character is important.

• *Pity the Poor Music Teacher* who has to write her staffs and notes on the chalkboard in each classroom she visits. If she uses an OHP, all she needs to do is make one transparency—and the drudgery is taken out of her work thereafter.

• *Scenery Making Can be Quite a Task,* unless you use an OHP. There are two methods, and one is the epitome of simplicity. All you need do is stretch a thin white bed sheet on an appropriately sized frame. Project a transparency through the back of the sheet, and you have your scenery.

In the second method, project your scenery transparency onto blank scenery frames and outline with a soft pencil. Then just fill in your outline in the desired colors.

• *If You Run Out of Special Carbons,* an adequate typewritten transparency can be made by typing an ordinary mimeograph stencil (with heavy pressure) and sandwiching it between 2 clear acetate sheets. Use only pica type or larger—preferably a primary typewriter size face.

• *A Visible Magnetic Field* is easy to produce for all to see. Just place a sheet of acetate on the projector stage. Then put a magnet on the acetate. Sprinkle iron filings over the magnet. A field will form—immediately visible on the screen.

Chapter Four

OPAQUE
PROJECTION

The Opaque Projector

The opaque projector has been the subject of controversy for years. Testimonials range from "wonderful" to "not very useful"—and both reactions have some merit. What you'll believe depends on your educational needs and point of view. An understanding of how the opaque projector operates will help you to realize how such widely divergent opinions can exist side-by-side.

Projector Characteristics. Opaque projection depends on the ability of an object to reflect light.

A high intensity projection lamp, usually a 1,000 watt incandescent, shines directly on the flat opaque object or picture. Light is reflected from the picture into a reversing mirror, which sends its light through the lens system to the screen.

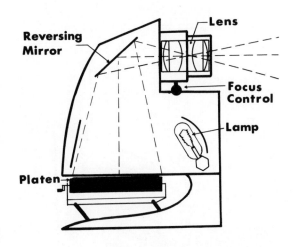

Fig. 4.1—Opaque projection depends on the reflective power of the opaque illustration or material placed in the projector. Since most opaque objects are not designed to be reflective, this type of projection is inefficient. Nevertheless, it is the only device which can project an opaque object or picture!

A blower must be incorporated into the projector to help dissipate the intense heat. Projector design is rather bulky, too, to further assist in the heat spreading process.

Focusing is easily accomplished by moving the lens in and out, usually with a rack and pinion gear system.

Most opaque projectors are equipped with an internal pointer system which projects an arrow onto the screen to assist the teacher in pointing out items of specific importance to her pupils. Pointer operation in the projectors which use a separate bulb (or pointer unit) is relatively simple. It is a trifle more difficult in models that use a mirror to project the arrow. If you wish, you can obtain, as accessory equipment, a separate, hand held pointer which allows you far greater convenience and flexibility.

All projectors make provision for adjusting projector elevation within fairly narrow limits.

Operation. The opaque projector usually has a platen which lowers to accept materials for projection. After the material is inserted, the platen is raised into position for projection. It will also have a locking device or will be spring-loaded to compensate for material thickness. Regardless of the thickness of the object being projected, the platen is designed to remain level since any tilting would cause distortion of the projected image. If the machine is equipped with a roller type platen, flat pictures can be inserted at the side and carried into the center of the platen by merely turning a crank.

After the platen has been raised to the desired level, switch on the projector and adjust the focus control.

Pictures are held in place during projection wither by an annealed plate glass pressure plate or by a forced air suction or pressure system.

One common problem which seems to plague many teachers who are unfamiliar with the opaque is that there is no image on the screen,

Fig. 4.2—Flat pictures, or even thicker 3 dimensional objects are easily inserted into the projector by lowering the platen. The platen is often equipped with a hold mechanism which will keep it at any desired opening so that thicker objects may be held at the proper level for projection.

although the copy to be projected has been inserted and the projection bulb is obviously on. This perplexing fault has three cures you can try:

1. Remove the lens cap.
2. Darken the room.
3. Move the projector closer to the screen.

The first solution, absurd as it may seem, is a common fault. Most visual devices do not have lens caps, so you might not look for one. But opaque projectors usually do. Take a look at yours!

The second answer "Darken the room" is also obvious, since ambient room light may completely obliterate the image from an opaque projector.

The third situation—closely related to the second—would probably occur only with your first attempt at opaque projection. Accidentally placing the projector too far away from the screen can result in an out of focus image so large that practically no light reaches the screen.

A fourth problem can also result in no light on the screen, but correction would require service. Some opaques use glass mirrors. If the reversing mirror should break—no light will reach the screen, and the mirror must be replaced. In modern machines the mirror is usually unbreakable.

If you want to be certain of getting an image on the screen, start the machine when it is about 5 feet from the screen. Then move it away slowly until the image is about the right size. Then focus, and you'll project properly.

Limitations. To one who has never used an opaque projector, the disadvantages of this bulky elephant of the AV jungle may seem to far outweigh any advantages.

Since light loss due to reflective projection is so great, the projected image—even in a completely darkened room—lacks the sharp, brilliant quality of a projected transparency.

High wattage lamps are used to compensate for the reflective loss, but even then, the 140 to 150 lumens placed on the screen is only $\frac{1}{15}$ the brilliance of overhead projection.

The opaque projector, therefore, *cannot be used successfully in a normally lighted classroom.* This factor severely limits its usefulness. However, if complete darkness is easy to achieve, the opaque can be a valuable teaching tool.

In an effort to squeeze out as much light as possible, opaque projector designers usually place the projection lamp close to the copy being projected. This can result in scorching the item being projected unless it is held down. The major problem of burning occurs on the pages of books which are not held down by a pressure plate.

Moving the platen to change the picture can cause another disturbing situation. Light bleeding from the projector when the platen is lowered can not only be distracting, but can even be momentarily blinding since the light at the platen is so much brighter than both the dark room and the projected image.

Advantages. With such a ponderous list of limitations, you might well wonder why you should use the opaque at all! There's one simple answer: *It's unique!* There is no other device which can project images from non-transparent materials!

This factor alone makes it an extremely important instructional aid. It means that:

1. No transparency preparation is needed. Actual printed, drawn, or photographed matter can be shown with no special preparation.
2. Small pictures are enlarged so that large groups can view at one time.
3. Cost of materials is insignificant. Pictures suitable for projection may be clipped from magazines and newspapers.
4. Projector operation is simple. Insert material, switch the opaque on, focus, and project!

Non-Instructional Opaque Projectors. Some purveyors offer for sale inexpensive ($5-$7) opaque projectors for which fantastic claims are made. One such advertisement proclaims "Casts sharp, giant enlargements . . . in brilliant color or black and white." Another says, "Enlarges any illustrated material up to four feet wide."

In reality, the enlargements of which this particular opaque projector is capable are hardly sharp or brilliant—unless you happen to be projecting in an unlit dungeon at midnight on a moonless night.

And the inference that the illustrated material may be up to 4 feet wide is clearly contradicted by a later statement—"Takes copy *up to* 3 by 3⅝ *inches.*"

Opaque Projection Tips

Mounting Pictures for Projection. Although techniques for picture mounting are covered extensively in Chapter 8, special consideration must be given to mounting for opaque projection.

If there is the possibility of prolonged projection, you should use a glue which will not be affected by the heat of the projection bulb.

Least suitable are rubber, wax, shellac, and thermoplastic base adhesives, for they all lose holding power under heat.

Of the commonly available adhesives, liquid "white glue" seems to hold up quite well under the opaque's heat stress.

Any adhesive is satisfactory, of course, if a cover sheet of annealed plate glass is placed over the picture being projected. This is the best method since it protects both the adhesive and the picture itself.

One other detail must be considered. In order to prevent curling or bubbling, due to air expansion and paper drying, pictures mounted for opaque projection should be completely adhered to the mount—not merely "spot glued."

Making "Paper Movies." The so-called "paper movie" is really a series of separate pictures which either tell a story or center about one common theme. The pictures are connected together with a flexible tape and folded at the tape joint in accordion style.

A Standard opaque projector can accept material which is up to 10″ x 10″. When you're making a paper movie the 10 inch length becomes critical. If the length is less than ten inches, more than one "frame" of your "movie" will appear since the projector automatically projects a 10 x 10 inch platen area. If your picture is more than 10 inches long, part of the frame will be lost, since it exceeds the aperture limit.

In use, the paper movie is run through the projector by turning the platen roll crank (or drawing the movie strip through manually if your projector doesn't have a roll platen). Allow only one frame at a time to be projected.

Topics and Types. Subjects for movies cover a wide range. The one thing to remember is that your pupils would probably like to take part in both planning and preparation for the project.

At primary grade levels, themes can be simple—community helpers, the weather, and the seasons are ideal subjects, as are leaves and

Fig. 4.3—Properly folded paper movies will roll easily through the projector when the platen crank is turned.

flowers. If your pupils haven't yet developed the ability to draw such things, magazines and catalogs have a wealth of such materials.

Middle and upper grade pupils can create more sophisticated movies. A story theme can run through it and a pupil committee can develop a narration script to provide information and continuity between scenes.

Another type of paper movie uses visual, rather than sound continuity. A social studies class made a time line on a 10″ wide strip of white shelving paper. Important dates were illustrated on 8″ square sheets of paper and pasted to the time line at appropriate points. The finished time line was rolled slowly through the opaque projector by a student operator who stopped at each illustration. The pupil who made the illustration became narrator and explained the event to the class. This type of continuous movie should be rolled in a large diameter circle rather than folded since the illustrations might not occur at exactly the ten inch intervals needed for folding.

Another type of continuous strip paper movie uses illustrations common to adjacent frames to achieve continuity. This can be accomplished without having to repeat any drawings by merely making the movie in the form of a frieze and advancing it about 8 inches instead of the usual 10. This will cause the picture which was at the right of one scene to be at the left of the succeeding one—thus providing visual continuity. Examples suitable for this type of presentation would be the skyline of our city or town, the street on which your school is situated, storefronts on the main street, and similar topics which could be expressed in a "panoramic" manner.

Sometimes a visual "device" can be used to establish continuity, though it is only incidentally part of the story. One class made a paper movie showing the peoples of the Earth, using as continuity a manned satellite whirling around the globe. The satellite was pictured in one frame as conveniently passing over a particular land mass. The next frame of the "movie" was a closeup of a child from that part of the world in traditional costume.

Other Visual Devices. *Postcard Travel.* In your vacation travels, be certain to gather an array of postcards. Their heavy stock will generally permit projection without excessive heat curl—especially if they are the printed rather than the photographic type.

Postcards are particularly useful in geography or history lessons. Although textbook pictures are fine, pupils prefer to see cards that you've actually gathered in places you visted personally.

English Compositions. Try analyzing pupil compositions for the entire class instead of merely correcting them outside of class time. With the help of the opaque, the entire page can be shown at one time. Then all pupils can benefit from the reasoning which prompted your corrections.

Music. If you have only one copy of a song, don't bother duplicating more for the whole class. Try using the opaque instead. All your pupils will be able to see—and sing—at the same time.

Murals. The opaque projector can slash large amounts of time from the task of mural making. Just follow this simple process.

Use a sheet of kraft paper, 36″ wide, in whatever length you need. Tack it over the length of the class bulletin board. Next draw a small sketch of the proposed mural on a sheet of paper which has the same length to width *proportions* as the mural paper. Project the drawing onto the kraft paper with the opaque projector. Outline the image with white chalk. Later the mural may be colored as desired with tempera or colored chalk. If chalk is used, be certain to spray the finished mural with a fixative (clear plastic).

Maps and Diagrams. It's often quite easy to obtain a desk size outline map, but large wall maps are often more difficult to secure. With the opaque you can reproduce large, accurately proportioned maps for a variety of uses.

At times, the use may be as much decorative as educational. One class used a small outline map to make a large permanent map of their state on the wall of the auditorium. The map was projected using the opaque and each county was painted with enamels. Place names were made with large press letters and sealed with shellac.

Chalkboard maps are easy to make, too, and, in the absence of printed wall maps, they can be excellent substitutes. Drawing chalkboard maps from opaque projected materials is an ideal pupil committee project. The outline should be made in a standard chalk, then colored, if needed. If a more permanent map is desired, just draw the map on a permanent material, such as a window shade, spray with clear plastic.

Other diagrams and line drawings can be made the same way.

Books and Magazines. Single copies of books can be shared with the whole class through the opaque projector. This is an especially valuable technique in telling stories to primary grade children. Seeing the projected book often encourages young children to "read" the book for themselves.

Some teachers find the opaque ideal for projecting prints of art masterpieces from museum catalogs.

Current affairs magazines provide another source for opaque

Fig. 4.4—Opaque projectors are valuable for enlarging pictures for group study. Most pictures would otherwise be suitable only for individual use. (*Charles Beseler Co.*)

materials, particularly for social studies classes. Together with newspapers, they provide the best—and often the only—source of current maps of emerging nations.

When books are projected, you must remember to use a pressure plate to hold the book in place.

Realia Projection. Although the opaque projector was designed for use with two-dimensional objects—many materials with shallow depth may be projected also.

Coins can be projected by merely placing them on the stage. Leaves are projectable, but should have a glass pressure plate on them. Fabrics can be used too, and only the most delicate need to be mounted.

The range of objects that you can use is vast—only two factors must be remembered—the materials must be able to withstand the heat and all must be approximately the *same thickness* in order that all will be in focus on the screen.

Of course, there is one time when you can use to good effect the fact that the opaque can only focus in one plane at one time. If you place items of different thicknesses on the platen, you can focus in on each thing individually—leaving the others out of focus, and thus less distracting. The same technique is used by photographers who allow the subject to be in focus, but cause the background to blur.

Stage Scenery and Props. Drawing lifesize objects freehand often presents difficulties for the uninitiated. But with the opaque projector, a small drawing can be blown up to full size. Scenery can be made on regular frames, or on inexpensive fiberboard panels. Scenery props can be projected onto chipboard. For example, one teacher needed statues of famous Americans as props in a class Memorial Day play. Pupils were given assignments to find line drawings of United States military heroes in various textbooks. Tracings were made and then were enlarged with the opaque onto gray chipboard, using a broad felt tip

78

flow pen. The resulting statues were cut out and mounted to stand erect with triangular cardboard backings.

Forms for All. Many teachers have discovered that the opaque can help them teach the proper way to fill out forms.

One librarian regularly instructed fourth grade children in filling out applications for library cards. Because of a high incidence of errors, she turned to the opaque so that she could discuss the application with her fourth graders before they actually filled them out.

United States Government forms and State forms, especially those pertaining to taxation, are ideal subjects for opaque use. Secondary business classes can use opaque enlargements where government supplied "blow ups" are not available.

In its one use—enlargement of opaque flat pictures and thin objects —the opaque has literally hundreds of applications. Try it when you have to make any picture larger!

Chapter Five

RADIO, TV,
AND SOUND SYSTEMS

To some teachers, it may appear that this chapter brings together an array of unlikely partners. But the reason is sound, for all three have one thing in common: the ultimate user seldom has much control over the instructional content of the media. In radio and television, the classroom teacher, practically speaking, has only one choice: to use or not to use. Accordingly, with radio and television, primary consideration will be given to the *use* aspect of the media, not to materials preparation. Since sound systems are being installed in most new school construction, there is an increasing possibility that you, as a classroom teacher, may move from the relatively passive role of listener, to the role of program writer or producer. It is interesting to note that essentially the same technical factors which are considered by broadcasters must be taken into account by the teacher who would use a sound system properly.

Television

Types. Television, as used in education, usually falls into one of these categories:

    a. Internal Classroom Use (closed circuit).
    b. Multiple Class instruction within a school building (closed circuit).
    c. Multiple Class instruction in multiple buildings (closed circuit or broadcast).
    d. Sponsored programs with educational value on Commerical Television (broadcast).
    e. Educational programs (or instructional ones) on Educational Television Channels (broadcast).
    f. Educational sustaining programs on Commercial Television, e.g. news, current affairs coverage, etc. (broadcast).

Internal Classroom Use TV. Teacher use of television in instruction will generally be as a demonstration device. It's a truly valuable tool for expanding the physical viewing limits of the classroom. If you've ever had the disconcerting experience of a mass of students crowding around you during a demonstration, you'll appreciate what TV can do. With television monitors strategically placed throughout the classroom, each pupil can have a front-row-center seat. And you, the teacher? Well you can demonstrate under the watchful eye of the TV camera.

Pupils no longer have to depend on chance for an opportunity to see what you're doing. And you don't have to wander about the room making certain that each pupil sees the rock, seed, leaf, or other small object.

If an experiment has any potential danger, you certainly wouldn't want a crowd of viewers close to it. But from a distance, they can't see! Unless you use a classroom TV.

Television isn't limited to classroom demonstration use. It can substitute for an overhead or an opaque projector, too.

To use the television for overhead transparency projection, the slide must be placed on a ground glass light box. The TV camera is mounted on a stand above the light box. Then you use the transparency

Fig. 5.1—The television camera moves in close during a demonstration and provides image magnification for better student viewing. (*ITV Center, San Jose State College*)

Fig. 5.2—One microscope and a television camera provide an enlargement big enough for class use. This is particularly important in microscopy since a group can view and discuss the *same* slide simultaneously. The TV microscope can be used in a lighted room, unlike the microprojector, which is suited only to a completely darkened area. (*Cohu Electronics, Inc.*)

just as you would on an overhead projector. The results are visible to your class on the TV monitors.

Use as an opaque projector is quite similar. The only difference is that you omit the light box and illuminate the object being shown instead.

The TV camera can help your school microscope to accommodate all eyes at once. The camera can easily be placed on a standard microscope eyepiece. Then your entire TV screen fills with the view in the microscope field.

As a classroom teaching tool, the TV has some limitations. Expense is great—certainly more than any other device to be used by the individual teacher. Also screen size—generally from 21 to 24 inch diagonal—limits the size of the resultant image. If the object being telecast is 2″ in diameter, then an increase to, say, 10 inches on a TV screen certainly improves viewing. But, if the object to be televised is a 2′ x 4′ map, then the necessary reduction to the size of the TV screen could make important detail too small to see!

Other Educational Television. In all other types of ETV the classroom teacher is very little involved, except to the extent of service or an advisory or planning committee. Rather, the "TV teacher" demonstrates, instructs directly, or provides supplementary enrichment material.

Although there has been a great deal of public concern over the possibility of television "replacing the teacher," the simple fact is that this is false! Where TV has been used instructionally, no one has been replaced. Rather, it has enabled school administrators to redeploy teachers in a manner which permits reducing class size pressures on pupils and teachers.

The satisfaction that both groups have experienced was shown in the report of the TV teaching program conducted in Montgomery County, Maryland, under a grant from the Fund for the Advancement of Education of the Ford Foundation. At the end of a year of instruction

Fig. 5.3—Instructional materials which are often unavailable to the classroom teacher must be used by the TV instructor. Greater preparation and precision are generally found in TV instruction. (*ITV Center, San Jose State College*)

by TV teachers, more than 90% of the classroom teachers and 98% of the students wanted to continue with TV instruction.

What part does the classroom teacher play in instructional television? The major functions are small group instruction, remedial instruction, or monitorial.

Where there is true *instruction* by the TV teacher, the classroom teacher becomes a member of an educational team. If, for example, your 6th grade class, together with the other two 6th grades in your school, is being taught science by television in one large room—one teacher serves the monitorial function of caring for all pupils in the TV room. The other teachers are then free to work with the pupils from other grades. Many other possibilities for time utilization exist, but use of such time profitably may require the modification of the "self-contained classroom" concept, and an understanding that TV need not be only a supplementary medium—it can be used for direct instruction too!

CCTV, Broadcast, or Microwave? When a telecast is intended solely for use within one classroom or building, distribution of the video signal presents but few problems—all of which may be solved locally with amplifiers and cables.

But once you broaden your transmission horizons to encompass multiple schools—an important decision becomes necessary. While the teacher will ordinarily have nothing to do with the selection of transmission method, a working knowledge of the systems will give you an appreciation of the problems involved in the distribution of that signal which reaches you by the mere flip of a switch.

Almost all true Closed Circuit Television (CCTV) distribution is provided by contract with your local telephone company. The contract is generally for a period of years. It is less expensive initially than broadcast TV, but it can be far more expensive over the decades, since the coaxial lines are forever *leased* from your telephone company. The coaxial CCTV is a service-free system, since your telephone company maintains all lines and booster amplifiers. Your sole concern is the studio TV camera equipment and receivers.

Broadcast ETV uses channels in the standard television broadcast bands, that is, channels 2 to 13 and 14 to 83 of the UHF and VHF bands. These channels are found on all home receivers manufactured after January 1, 1965.

Another type of electromagnetic radiation instructional television was made available in 1963, when the Federal Communications Commission announced allocation of 31 television channels for instructional purposes. Since they lie in the frequency range of 2500 to 2686 mega-cycles, where the wavelength is extremely small, this is known as micro-wave television. Four microwave channels may be allotted to any one institution.

The limitation of any one geographic area to one educational sta-tion in the VHF range and precious few more in the UHF, meant that Broadcast ETV was useful only for the most general type of educational fare. With the advent of microwave instructional television, signals could be beamed from the transmitter to each school—and no one else would receive them. In essence, then, microwave TV is a closed circuit system transmitted selectively through the airwaves. Like CCTV on coaxial cables, 4 channel microwave TV can enable a school district to telecast a full schedule to all grade levels with as many as a hundred programs in a school day.

Commercial TV as an Educational Aid. Some educational functions are served by commercial broadcast TV stations—either by design or accident.

Providing educational content most certairly is not the primary goal of a commercial television station. However, stations are literally bludgeoned into providing such service by FFC requirements that a "reasonable" amount of broadcast time be devoted to "sustaining time." Translated, this means that a station *must* provide public service pro-gramming, or risk the loss of license renewal. Sustaining time broad-casting is usually of a current affairs, news, educational, or religious nature.

Very little commercial programming is instructional. The few ex-cursions into direct instruction—"Continental Classroom," "Sunrise Se-mester," and the like—were well received by viewers, but were rele-gated by networks to unlikely early morning or late evening hours.

But commercial television is the best source of one type of educa-tional programming. Never in history has better, more instantaneous news coverage been given the public. Teachers especially should make use of public affairs programs. Election coverage, Presidential talks, a coverage of visits of dignitaries can only be provided by broadcast com-mercial television. When you use such programs, make certain your students understand the reasons for using it.

From time to time, the program will, of course, be interrupted by commercials. You should abide by your local school policy in regard to commercials. Most administrators realize that with the "sweet" we must accept the "bitter." A few demand that no commercials be viewed by students, so be prepared to control volume and brightness.

Using Broadcast TV in the Classroom. Broadcast television is largely *supplemental* to classroom instruction. This means that the classroom teacher retains fully his instructional functions, and must consider:

1. Coordination of classroom instruction with TV schedules. Unfortunately, the instantaneous nature of the television medium requires you to use it at the moment it is transmitted—or not use it at all. Low priced video tape recorders may change the picture if mass production takes place. However, it's doubtful that a school quality recorder will ever be low enough in price to let it compete with the ubiquitous motion picture projector.

2. Obtain a Program Guide, wherever possible. Companies which sponsor educationally valuable television programs often provide Teacher Guides which are available for the asking. They list goals of the program, an outline of the topic, and hints for program utilization.

3. Proper Viewing means class preparation. Unlike a motion picture, you can't show a television program over again. You can't stop in the middle for discussion. So students must clearly understand that total application to viewing is essential. Often the knowledge that an evaluation quiz will follow the program enhances the attention factor. If you have a Teacher's Guide, you might discuss high points of content even before the telecast. However, do not give pupils written questions in advance of the broadcast for this might detract from attention given to the program.

Television Receivers. School reception equipment falls into three categories: (1) video monitors, (2) RF receivers, and (3) combination units.

For most purposes, radio frequency receivers (RF) are similar to home television sets. Video monitors are used only in closed circuit wired systems and for camera monitoring purposes. Obviously, if your school has or will have a closed circuit television system, the most practical unit to purchase is the combination unit, which incorporates the ability to reproduce both video monitor and RF signals. Microwave instructional TV uses a converter to allow the signal to be reproduced on a standard broadcast receiver.

Receivers which are built especially for classroom use incorporate many safety features which are unavailable in home receivers.

Receiver Tuning. Some teachers greet TV controls with about the same enthusiasm as they would the bubonic plague. And many have good reason. Failure to understand basic control operation often causes severe knob twisting and results in a screen pattern worthy of a fabric designer!

On most RF television sets there are basic controls with which the user must be familiar:

1. On-Off Volume. A volume control is often incorporated with a power switch.

2. Brightness. Set about halfway from its counterclockwise (minimum) position.

3. Contrast. Sometimes called the "picture" control, this should be initially set at mid-position too.

4. Channel Selector. Set at desired channel index.

5. Fine Tuning. Rotate in either direction until clearest picture and sound are obtained.

6. Vertical Hold. If the picture on the screen appears to be rolling vertically, adjust this control until there is a single image without vertical movement.

7. Horizontal Hold. If the picture has diagonal or horizontal slashes, adjust the horizontal hold in either direction until a stationary picture is obtained. The horizontal hold is seldom found as a "front panel" control, so you should be familiar with its location.

The brightness and contrast controls interact, and may need further adjustment. If it requires extremely critical tuning to hold either vertical or horizontal circuits in synchronization, the receiver should be serviced, since proper operation allows a rather broad range of correct synchronization control settings.

If your set seems to be working (you have a lighted screen, but no image or sound), keep in mind that your school may have a master amplifier attached to the antenna. This means that you may be plugged into your antenna receptacle, but no signal gets to your receiver because the master amplifier is off. Before you ask that a set be serviced, make certain that your antenna amplifier is turned on!

TV Receiver Size and Placement. In classroom use the 23″ receiver size is generally considered adequate. Students should be seated at least 4 times the screen diagonal measurement away from the set. Some experts feel that the maximum viewing distance is about 15 times the screen size. You should be extremely hesitant about accepting such advice unless you stress the word *maximum.* Your students are likely to have a great deal of difficulty viewing small letters on the screen from a 30 foot distance.

While television producers try to take letter size into account by having relatively few words with large letters, the simple fact remains that a 23″ screen is just not large enough to show all the caption material

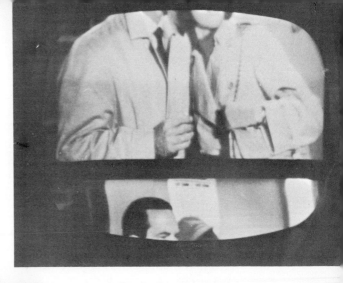

Fig. 5.4—When the television image has lost its vertical synchronization, the picture will begin to roll vertically, with a black bar appearing periodically. This can usually be corrected by adjustment of the Vertical Hold Control.

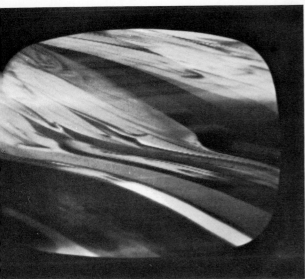

Fig. 5.5—A diagonal slashing of the image usually indicates the loss of horizontal synchronization. The condition is generally remedied by adjustment of the Horizontal Hold Control, which may not be a front panel control.

Fig. 5.6—Correct typing technique of the teacher may be shown simultaneously to all pupils on closed circuit TV. By the standard method, no more than four or five students could view comfortably, and then, only with a great deal of classroom commotion. (*Litton Educational Technology Division/ Litton Industries*)

which might be needed, in a size which could be read by pupils 30 feet from the screen.

There's only one way to compensate for this television limitation: moving in for closer viewing. This reduces the number of pupils who can view the screen without crowding too close together.

Obviously, ideal set placement would let each student view comfortably from his own seat. About 20 to 25 students can ordinarily be accommodated by one 23″ set. To make certain that all your students can distinguish all legends on the television screen, you should view it from the same distance as the farthest pupil.

The receiver itself should be placed so that no light falls directly on the face of the picture tube. The so-called "black" on a TV screen is no darker than the face of the tube when the set is shut off. So, if you let light fall on the screen—especially sunlight—the picture will lose contrast and appear "washed out."

Nor should the receiver be placed with its back to a window, for this would result in students facing the glare of the outdoors. The set should be high enough for all pupils to view without obstruction—usually from three to six feet above the floor. Special wide base stands should be used if sets are to be mobile.

Radio

Educational radio serves many levels of instruction. It is widely used in adult education, brings school to deep rural areas, and serves as a training ground for college students majoring in communications. But of primary concern to us as teachers is the broadcast of programs especially designed for classroom use.

Operators of these stations are most often universities, states, or other governmental units. Unfortunately, extremely few stations are owned by

Fig. 5.7—Champion spellers in a student radio quiz program, *Spelldown*, are awarded the fruits of their victories by Franklyn Titus, Deputy Superintendent of Newark Schools. (*WBGO, Newark (N.J.) Board of Education*)

local boards of education and thereby programmed especially for the school district. Rather, programming is largely of the "general interest" type, and suffers from trying to be all things to all men. The few school districts which own and operate their own radio stations are able to program directly for the curriculum of the district—and they do.

Uses of Educational Radio. The most important reason for the existence of non-commercial educational radio is found in its application to the specific educational needs of its intended audience. Of secondary importance is the valuable training received by students who engage in radio workshops which produce education programs.

Commercial radio stations cater to listener tastes. Educational radio must consider both tastes and needs, and often include offerings in these areas:

1. Grade level news and current events programs. These are usually quizzes, discussions, interviews with newsmakers, or dramatizations. Their use in class can be as a culmination or review of the week's news. Some stations broadcast quizzes to listeners for them to answer so they may determine how well pupils have retained broadcast information. The format used on the broadcast can serve as a model for your classroom current events period.

2. Language Arts. Your pupils can be awakened to the world of literature by radio. Some stations use the device of having pupils discuss their favorite books on the air. Good readers, pupils and teachers alike, read selections or adaptions from literature. Slow learners, or pupils with limited reading ability especially profit from such programs.

Radio writing is an English experience which educational radio stations foster through workshops. Certainly the ideal is reached when pupils can hear their own writings, or those of their classmates, produced or read on the air.

Storytelling by radio is another English experience which is particularly valuable at lower grade levels.

Library programs have been found valuable too. Lectures, book reviews, and dramatic interpretations keep the availability of library resources continually before the public.

In your own class, pupils can write and produce their own dramatizations or other programs modeled on that which they've heard on the air.

3. Social Studies. Radio provides a means of getting local information to your pupils with a minimum of expense. Local and state history, industry, and government are topics particularly suited to radio presentation.

Interviews with leaders of business or government, and dramatizations about distant lands and people help pupils gain an expanding knowledge of the world about them.

In addition, programs encouraging good citizenship are regular fare on educational radio.

4. Art and Music. There can be no question about the suitability of music for radio presentation, since radio is but a vehicle for carrying sound. Long years of experience have proved that actual music instruction can be accomplished via radio. Many classroom teachers experience difficulty in teaching vocal music, and few will deny that instruction by an expert radio music teacher is far superior to instruction by a non-musically inclined classroom teacher. And the value of such instructional broadcasts in rural areas is self-evident!

Music appreciation can be held at the students' own level on radio. Programs which would be prohibitive if done "live" at each school are economically sound when performed for vast radio audiences. Some sponsored programs, such as the California Oil Company's "Classroom Concert Hall" bring outstanding artists to children in a manner which appeals to their age level.

An interesting art experience is possible in your own classroom during a music appreciation program. Give your students a sheet of drawing paper, crayon, and instructions to draw whatever the music impels them to create. The results are often spectacular! Some can even be used for a display of spontaneous art.

5. Science, Health and Safety. In science, direct instruction is possible by radio, and advance preparation is generally needed. Pupils can be instructed to bring simple objects to school for use during the science broadcast (or after the broadcast).

Safety and Health topics can be treated effectively by radio dramatizations, and the topics treated on the air can then be more fully developed in the classroom.

Radio, from the standpoint of the teacher, is primarily a supplementary device. Anything which can be done via radio, can also be done via recording—but at greater cost and with less immediacy. Any program broadcast could also have been provided on a record, but then you'd have to contend, for example, with a news broadcast many weeks late. There is an aura about the fact that a program is broadcast which makes it important to pupils.

Radio Reception. Educational radio transmission may be of two types—Amplitude Modulation (AM) or Frequency Modulation (FM).

The latter is almost exclusively used in the United States, so the teacher who would use educational radio should have some knowledge about FM.

High fidelity reproduction is possible from an FM broadcast signal since the Federal Communications Commission requires that all broadcast equipment be capable of handling audio modulation from 50 to 15,000 cycles. However, the frequency range reproduced in your classroom is limited by the characteristics and design of your FM receiver. If, for example, you use a table model radio with a 4 inch loudspeaker, you'll *never* reproduce a flat response curve of 50-15,000 cycles. It's the old story: A chain is no stronger than its weakest link.

If your receiver will be used for music reception, be certain that it meets *your* minimum standards, even if it can't reproduce the 50-15,000 cycle range. But if the radio will be used exclusively for speech reproduction, there is little justification for embarking onto the added expense of music quality equipment.

When it's properly tuned, FM radio is almost static free. Static has a tendency to ride the envelope of a carrier wave. In AM, the envelope contains the needed modulation, so it must be reproduced by the radio —static and all! In FM, however, the carrier amplitude remains relatively constant. Static still rides the tips of the carrier wave, but with FM, the tips of the carrier are clipped off since the audio modulation intelligence in FM is a function of *frequency* variation, which has nothing to do with the carrier amplitude. Result: you get crisp, clear, static free sound.

There is one annoying characteristic found in some FM receivers— drift. But fortunately it can be controlled. Be certain that your radio has an automatic frequency control (AFC) circuit built into it. Ordinarily this will be evidenced by a front panel switch station "AFC," though it is possible for a receiver to have the circuit but not have the switch. AFC tends to hold your radio tuned to the carrier frequency of the station.

In tuning to an FM station, be as accurate as you possibly can, for critical tuning improves reception immeasurably. It is far more important than critical AM tuning.

All FM radios work *best* with an external antenna. In areas of high signal strength (near the transmitter), you'll probably have so much signal that you'll be satisfied with the radio's internal antenna, or with no antenna at all. But in distant areas, an antenna is essential.

An added convenience you should consider in the purchase of any radio receiver for school use is an audio output jack. This will allow you to record directly from the radio to a tape recorder without a microphone. It provides better recorded sound quality than that obtained by the loudspeaker to microphone method.

Radio Listening. Certainly an educationally profitable experience can result from proper listening. However, it would be a grievous error to assume that pupils are truly listening merely because they have the ability to hear. Good listening habits must be developed.

The first step is the elimination of distractions. Desks should be cleared of all items which could divert attention from the broadcast. There was much merit in the oft used statement of the teacher you remember so well from your childhood, "Now get into your best listening positions."

Added concentration may be gained by using directed study questions. They can be written on the chalkboard for viewing during the broadcast, but pupils should not be allowed to answer questions in writing during the broadcast. Note taking should be held to an absolute minimum, limited to listing major points for post-broadcast discussion.

Above all, don't assume that learning has taken place. If it's worth listening to, it's worth discussion and evaluation.

Sound Systems

Central Sound Systems are installed in most new school construction. While the prime reason for installation is admittedly administrative, inter classroom-office communication, it can also be used for instructional purposes.

Ideally, a soundproof room should be available in each school. This "studio" should be separated from the "control" room by a double glass partition. Unfortunately, even in new schools not more than a handful meet the ideal.

But, as long as an audio signal from one part of the building may be amplified and sent to loudspeakers in classrooms, the central sound system can be a teaching tool. Transmission to classrooms must be selective, however, for not all programs are suitable for all grade levels.

The sample program shows the uses to which a central sound system may be put.

Programs which originate on local sound are locally produced in the school. They generally include:

1. *School News and Announcements.* Although the administrator will most often make announcements, this period can provide an excel-

lent opportunity for live participation by pupils. Students who are selected as announcers should be well rehearsed before a microphone prior to actual "broadcast." Suitable news items would include announcements of auditorium presentations, winners of intramural sports activity, or even community happenings of interest to the student body.

2. *Skits and "radio" drama.* Pupil written and produced programs can serve many purposes. Short skits can be used to advertise fund appeals, school shows and sport events. Longer "radio" type drama may be recorded on tape and presented to selected other classes.

Scripts written by pupils should be models of good English. This activity shows a practical aspect of language usage, and students should be made to realize that only their best efforts should be shared with others.

3. *Music.* Some schools use pupil produced choral programs for "broadcast" to all parts of the school, especially during the Christmas holiday season or before patriotic holidays.

4. *Playground.* Music can be used as background for playground and physical education activities, including skating, dancing and exercises.

Whatever can be done via radio for an entire school system can be accomplished for the individual school via a central sound system. Don't let it be a mere announcement device.

Chapter Six

RECORDS
AND RECORDERS

In 1877, Thomas A. Edison produced the first practical recording. Since that time, millions of records have been produced. They fall into two primary categories: mechanical and magnetic. Within these groups, you can find discs, tapes, belts, cylinders, wires, and other substances on which knowledge is recorded. In educational use, most magnetic recordings are on tape, and most mechanical recordings are on discs.

Disc Recordings

The actual making of a mechanical disc recording, or record, is a complex technique which will, in all probability, never be attempted by most classroom teachers. Still, to understand what happens when you use a record in your classroom, you should be familiar with the disc recording technique—if only from a reading acquaintance standpoint.

How a Disc Recording is Made. Sound, generally in the form of speech or music, is converted into electrical waves by the microphone. These waves, which vary in direct relation to the original sound, are amplified and made to vary a diamond tipped needle mounted in a "cutting head." Some heads vary the needle vertically and result in a vertical (hill and dale) recording groove. The transcription, used by radio stations, is an example of the vertical record. Most American discs, however, are cut laterally; and home and school equipment are generally not designed to play vertical cuts.

The master recording itself is most often cut on a soft, easily damaged lacquer coated aluminum disc. From this master, a mold is made, and subsequent discs are "pressings" made from a mold of the master recording. This system has given us mass produced discs, inexpensively priced.

Discs. Today's records are classified by speed and size. The amount of recording time on a disc, within limits, is related to speed of rotation, groove width, and record diameter. The four standard speeds are 78, 45, 33⅓ and 16⅔ revolutions per minute (RPM).

78 RPM. The oldest of these speeds is the 78 RPM disc. Since grooves are relatively wide and the record turns rapidly, standard 10 or 12 inch 78 records can only accommodate 3 to 5 minutes of recording time per side. Older records are made of brittle plastic and break easily. Improvement in record quality over the years can easily be demonstrated by playing a pre-World War II disc and then comparing its sound to a present-day record.

45 RPM. These discs, often referred to as EP (extended play) have a 7″ diameter and a wide center spindle hole. Recording grooves are about half the width of standard 78 records, so twice as much recording time can be had per radial inch. However, since the discs are only 7″ in diameter, recording time for the 45 disc remains at 3 to 5 minutes.

33⅓ RPM. While the first 45 RPM manufacturer selected that speed and spindle so that only his playback equipment could be used, the manufacturer who popularized the 33⅓ RPM disc did exactly the opposite. It was made to conform in speed to the 33⅓ wide groove electrical transcription used by radio stations. This meant that no substantial change in turntable equipment would be needed to play a new microgroove LP (long playing) disc. This new record was originally 12″, but special purpose microgroove discs have been made in a variety of sizes—with only the speed remaining constant. The 12″ LP can accommodate up to 15 minutes of recording time per side.

16⅔ RPM. The least common type standard disc is the "ultra-microgroove," often called the "talking book." Up to ½ hour of recording time is squeezed onto one side of a 7″ wide spindle disc. The sound quality possible with ultra-microgroove is somewhat less than the extremely high quality obtainable with the EP or LP 33⅓ RPM microgroove variety. However, ultra-microgroove is entirely adequate for speech use—as in the talking book.

The Stylus

Playback Styli. Many teachers who use the phonograph find that their greatest problem is the stylus—or needle, as it is more commonly called. Almost all styli used in schooltype phonographs are tipped in

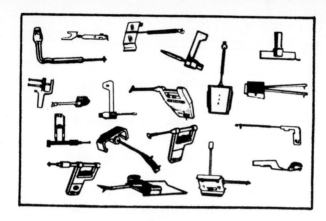

Fig. 6.1–Phonograph styli are made in many shapes. Each is designed to fit a particular cartridge. Replacement styli should be exactly the same as the original in size, shape, and characteristics.

diamond or sapphire. A few are made of metals, such as osmium, but these are extremely impractical for classroom use since the tip wears rapidly, demanding frequent change.

How To Select a Stylus. In order to select a stylus that meets your needs, you need to know about their characteristics. The diamond tip will give the most play before it must be discarded. Sapphire comes next, and metal tips last. But the very advantage which gives the diamond stylus its long life—hardness—also makes it the stylus which can wear down soft record grooves most easily.

Actually, any well shaped stylus will cause a minimum of record wear. The real problem occurs when, due to use, the stylus becomes worn. Then it acts like a chisel gouging its way through the grooves.

If you would give discs the care they deserve, change the stylus when the recommended number of plays has been met. If there's no way to tell this, then use a stylus microscope or shadowgraph periodically, to make certain that the stylus is not worn excessively. By either inspection method the worn stylus will show a flattened side rather than a rounded tip.

In playing a record, the stylus must "track" correctly—that is, it must ride in the groove with only enough pressure to keep it there through all its undulations. This stylus pressure varies for different tone arms and cartridges, but it should usually be from about 2 to 10 grams —and never more than 15. Unfortunately, tracking pressure is exceeded in most phonographs; and this always results in excessive record and stylus wear.

A common misconception is that all points are the same—only the mounts vary. A stylus must ride approximately midway into the groove. If the stylus tip is too broad, it will ride the peaks, and probably cause the arm to jump from groove to groove—often resulting in a scratch across the grooves. If the stylus is too thin, it will rest in the bottom of the groove. When it does, even an excellent disc sounds noisy.

Replacing a Stylus. When replacing a stylus, follow the cartridge manufacturer's recommendation. But, if you haven't replacement part lists handy, the following average guide may be followed:

Record Type	Preferred Stylus Size
78 rpm standard	3 mil
33⅓ rpm transcription	3 mil
33⅓ rpm LP microgroove	1 mil
45 rpm EP microgroove	1 mil
Stereo microgroove	.5 to .7 mil
16⅔ ultra-microgroove	.25 mil

Although the .25 mil stylus is best for use with ultra-microgroove recordings, it is almost impossible to obtain. The .5 or .7 mil stereo stylus can generally provide acceptable, if not optimum, results.

Most phonographs provide two styli, available for use alternately by a "turnover" or switching system. However, since at least four different size styli are needed for best results with all types of standard recordings, any needle selection you use—presuming the use of all types of records— is a compromise.

Most dual needle stereo phonographs are equipped with a 3 mil needle, for 78 RPM discs, which is generally marked "78" or "STD"; and with a .7 or .5 mil stylus for Stereo, LP, and EP records. This latter stylus is usually marked "ST," "LD," or "MG." Monophonic dual needle cartridges usually contain a 3 mil stylus for 78 RPM records, and a 1 mil needle for all microgroove discs. This latter needle is only marginally suited for talking book 16⅔ RPM records.

Fig. 6.2A—Using a small jeweler's screwdriver, remove the screw which holds the stylus in place. If your cartridge uses another system of retention —such as a small thumb screw—loosen whatever holds the stylus in place. Remove the stylus. In some cartridges, only a pressure fit is used, in which case withdrawal with a slight extra pressure is all that's needed.

Fig. 6.2B—Carefully insert the replacement needle into the cartridge, following the same steps as removal, but in reverse order.

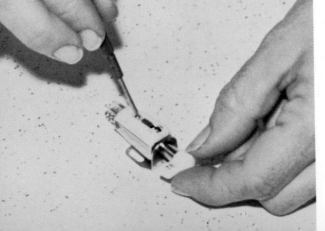

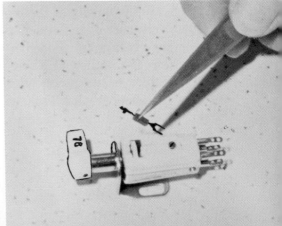

The most frequent cause of classroom phonograph failure is improper handling of the tone arm, which contains the styli. Bent, twisted, crushed, or even lost styli can make phonographs inoperative. But you don't have to send yours off to the repair shop for stylus troubles. Be prepared in advance by purchasing replacement styli before you need them.

It's easy to determine what replacement styli you need. The cartridge to which the stylus is attached is generally labelled with letters, numbers, color codes, or a combination thereof. Copy down the designation and take it to a local electronics parts supplier or write to a mail order supplier. It's a good idea to bring with you a drawing, or even better, the stylus itself, when you make the purchase. If there is any doubt, make exchange a condition of purchase.

Actual replacement of the stylus usually involves only adjustment of a screw or pressure fitting which holds the needle in place.

Theory of Operation. The latent audio intelligence pressed into a disc recording must be converted back to sound, if it is to be of instructional value.

The conversion process is essentially the reverse of recording. At the end of the phonograph's "tone arm" is a "cartridge" to which the stylus is attached. The cartridge is capable of converting mechanical vibration into corresponding electrical variations which can then be amplified and made into sound. Early acoustical phonographs converted the needle's vibration directly into sound, but this system was little more than a novelty without provision for sound amplification.

The phonograph needle, which is an integral part of the cartridge, vibrates in compliance with the impressions in the record groove. This motion is converted into a small electrical signal, usually by piezoelectric or magnetic means. When amplified and fed into a loudspeaker or earphones, the electrical signal becomes a reproduction of the original sound.

Phonograph Selection

The quality of the reproduced sound is limited by the capability of every part of the system. High quality recordings, cartridge, amplifier, and speaker are needed if you must have high fidelity sound reproduction. But must you? There is a strong tendency to call everything "hi-fi" (which means practically nothing) and to demand such performance. If a phonograph is to be used for music reproduction, then certainly you need the best you can afford, since the range of frequencies to be reproduced is quite wide. But if music is not an important factor, consider the fact that speech frequencies cover a very limited range which can be reproduced adequately by most inexpensive school-type phonographs.

Basic Needs. What should you look for in a school phonograph? If it is to be used by pupils, or moved from place to place, it definitely should be sturdily built, as most school or industrial use phonographs are. Such "luxuries" as metal luggage glides and corners on the case are really essentials.

From a safety standpoint, there is one major consideration, which ordinarily need not be considered in school-type equipment, but which must be considered in home equipment purchased for school use. The phonograph should have a power transformer, not an AC-DC circuit. The importance of this factor can't be overstressed. A power transformer successfully isolates the amplifier chassis from the power line—thus preventing a possible situation which could result in severe shocks or electrocution. Summed up, here's the best advice: Make certain the phonograph you use contains a power transformer if it plugs into an AC power line. As with any electrical equipment, grounded 3 prong plugs insure the greatest safety against equipment shock hazard.

Speeds. Almost all phonographs now produced have four fixed speeds, 16⅔, 33⅓, 45, and 78 RPM. Better quality machines include some means of varying speed above and below the nominal fixed speed. Good sound reproduction depends on correct turntable speed. Since voltage fluctuation can cause speed changes, some measurement and control should be provided.

Measurement is accomplished by stroboscopic means. The strobe disc may be placed on the phonograph turntable and the turntable allowed to revolve at the nominal selected speed. Since the arm and stylus may cause some "drag" and resultant lower turntable speed, strobe measurements should be taken under actual conditions—with record and arm in use. An alternating 60 cycle light is shone on the revolving strobe disc. If the turntable speed is correct, the printed bars on disc of the appropriate speed circle will appear to stand still. Suitable light is emitted from neon or fluorescent lamps connected to a 60 V. power source (most American home and school power receptacles qualify). Some phonographs have strobe test lights and strobe marks built into the machine itself. However, these devices are usually able to check correct rotation at one speed, not at all four.

Tone Arm. The tone arm should be light enough so that it does not exert any damaging pressure on the disc. If the phonograph is to be used on all types of records, including 16⅔ rpm talking books, the tone arm should have a plug in type cartridge since, as explained earlier, a non-standard, very narrow stylus is best for use on the talking book disc. Tone arm needle pressure can be measured on an inexpensive gauge designed for the purpose. Provision should always be made for locking the tone arm when not in use to prevent accidental stylus damage when the record player is carried from place to place. Better phonos will have a screw-type lock, but the spring clip found on less expensive types is generally adequate.

Provision should be made for a finger-type tone arm lift so that you can raise the arm from the record without any chance of damage to the record. Some manufacturers incorporate this feature as part of the arm locking device.

Turntable. The turntable itself is important in maintaining constant speed. Professional turntables are quite heavy to provide a speed governor effect. In most phonographs the rotation of the turntable is not that of the motor. Rather, drive is provided by a capstan wheel, on the motor's shaft, which, in turn, spins idler wheels that revolve the turntable. Usually these wheels engage only when fixed speed setting is in use. Since these wheels must make firm contact with the motor shaft and the turntable rim, they have a tendency to flatten at the point of contact. If the drive mechanism is left engaged during long hours of non-use the wheels will flatten, and you'll get the characteristic "thump, thump" sound during turntable rotation. Rather than be involved in expensive repair, it would be wise to follow manufacturers' recommendations as to the position of the fixed speed switch during non-use.

The turntable should also be at least as large as the largest record intended for use on it. If a 12″ disc is the maximum size to be used, then the turntable should be at least 12″ in diameter. Often manufacturers will advertise a phonograph as a "transcription" player—but the turntable is only 10″ or 12″—not the transcription 16″, or 17¼″ of a master. It is true, transcriptions can be played on a smaller turntable, but speed accuracy could be lost since there must be no slippage between record and turntable. Unless all of the record rests securely on the turntable, slippage could occur.

The center of any manual turntable should be equipped with a "pop-up" type of wide spindle to accommodate 45 RPM and 16⅔ RPM records. Without the pop up spindle you must have recourse to "spiders" —which convert the record hole to ¼″—or "adapters" which convert the spindle to the wide size. Spiders are most inconvenient, and loose wide spindle adapters are easily lost. Insist on the "pop-up" type.

Pause Controls. In educational use, there is often need to pause in mid-record, then to continue later from the same point. The most effective type of pause control puts an immediate brake somewhere in the drive system—usually the rim of the turntable itself. Other systems allow the arm to be lifted slightly off the surface of the record—allowing the turntable to continue its revolutions, but no sound to be emitted. When you wish to resume playing, the arm is allowed to return to the record—theoretically in the same groove it left. In actual practice, consistent results with this latter system are impossible. If critical stopping and starting are important—the turntable or drive system brake are the best devices—since they allow the needle to remain in the same record groove. If your phonograph doesn't have a pause control, you can use the old disc-jockey system. Put your finger on the edge of the record with sufficient force to overcome the friction which causes the record to turn with the turntable. With most machines, the disc will stop—but the turntable will continue to revolve.

Output. Every phonograph will have a built in loudspeaker or output jacks for external speakers. It's a good idea to have external speaker, and earphone jacks on any phonograph you buy. External extension speakers enable you to put the sound where you need it—generally well distributed throughout the room. In classroom use, one of the major problems of the internal speaker phonograph is that it is generally too loud for nearby pupils and too soft for those at the most distant part of the room. Multiple speakers can be distributed so as to compensate for this drawback. This cannot be done, however, when you are using stereo for stereo phonograph loudspeakers must be dual only, and critically spaced, to give a stereophonic effect.

Extension speakers must be electrically "matched" to the amplifier if they are to give maximum power transfer and fidelity. You can't just take any speaker you have around, attach it, and get proper reproduction. True—good fortune may be with you and all may work well—but don't depend on it. Speaker matching is measured in ohms of impedance and power in watts. If you do buy an extension speaker, be sure to tell your supplier that its impedance must match the amplifier output. You can usually get proper matching by using speaker equipment made by your phonograph manufacturer—though it's not always so!

When the output signal is fed to a set of headphones, impedance is also important. But it is all too often disregarded. Instead of labeling equipment in terms of specific impedance, manufacturers often simply state "high impedance" or "low impedance"—both of which mean very little, but are better than no labeling at all.

Inputs. Some phonographs make provision for the use of their amplifiers as a public address system. All that's needed is a microphone. Just as with output devices, the microphone impedance should match the input impedance.

Controls. Other than those already mentioned, a phonograph will always have an on-off and volume switch—usually incorporated into one control. As price increases, so does the number of controls. You may also have a "tone" control, which changes the tone from treble to bass or vice versa. Often treble and bass will be two separate but interacting controls. On stereo sets you'll also have a balance control to equalize sound from each stereo channel. For each microphone input there should be a separate control. In extremely expensive units you may even find some designated "expansion," "compression," and "brilliance." These are merely rather fine adjustments of the audio curve to create greater realism. Ordinarily they are not on school-type equipment.

Audio Distribution Boxes. Jack boxes will increase the flexibility of any record player by allowing multiple private earphone listening with only one output jack on your phonograph. The jack box serves to place many headphones in electrical parallel with the output jack of the phonograph. While small group jack boxes can be used without difficulty, large numbers—say classroom quantities—should be installed professionally by an audio engineer so that a severe impedance mismatch, with its resultant power loss and distortion, will not be created.

Record Care. Modern vinyl plastic records develop high static charges which attract dust; and a coating of dust becomes an abrasive which ruins the fine grooves of a microgroove record under the grinding

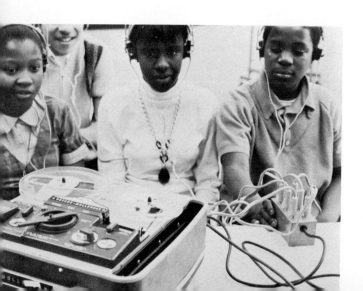

Fig. 6.3—When a multiple jack box is used, a group of children may listen to a recorded lesson and not disturb the rest of the class with the sound. The jack box cord is plugged into the recorder output jack, and pupil headphones are then plugged into the jack box. (*A. Winegarden*)

pressure of a stylus. Static is developed quite easily. Merely inserting the record into its sleeve creates static. Anti-static fluids and sprays are available which tend to reduce static, and brushes can be used to remove dust.

Records should always be stored vertically, away from heat. They should never be stacked, one on the other or piled on a slant. If a record has a sleeve (album) it should be kept in it since the cover provides needed rigidity.

Operation. Operation of a standard disc playback is extremely simple. If the volume control is separate from the amplifier on-off switch, set it almost at its lowest position, then turn the amplifier switch on. If both are in one control, switch it on, then leave volume near its lowest point. Newest solid state (transistor) amplifiers do not require any warmup time. By setting up your equipment at the lowest possible sound level, you can avoid distracting pupils with unnecessarily loud noises.

Next, check to see that the proper stylus will contact the record. If you have a multiple needle cartridge, changing styli is merely a matter of flipping a lever at the cartridge.

Set the motor speed control at the proper setting for the record you intend to use. Record speed is printed on the label of all standard recordings. Then place the record carefully on the turntable. Hold the disc by the edges. Never let your fingers touch the record grooves, since the oils from your fingerprints will hold the static attracted dust and considerably shorten the record's life.

Lift the tone arm and gently place it down on the record's lead cut—which is usually on the outer edge of the disc. In a very few instances, you may come across a record cut inside-out. Then the lead cut would be near the middle of the disc. This type of record is usually an older, individually cut master. Nevertheless, if you ever stumble on a recording which, when the tone arm is placed on the groove at the edge of the disc, merely goes round and round in the same groove—you've probably found an inside-out record!

Be extremely careful to place the arm on the record *gently,* and *straight down.* A sideward sweeping action could result in your accidentally cutting across the grooves. At best, this will result in a click during each revolution; at worst, the record becomes useless as the needle will refuse to stay in the recorded grooves, but will follow your new "side sweep" groove instead.

Accidentally switching the turntable on or off, changing speed mid-record, or playing a record at the wrong speed, does no great harm to the recording—but the resulting sound will probably be offensive to the ear, and, in the latter two instances, could result in accidental use of the wrong needle.

Magnetic Disc Records. Some flexible plastic discs, looking to the naked eye like standard disc recordings, are actually discs with unrecorded grooves which merely serve as a channel for a magnetic head at the end of a standard looking tone arm. This type of recorder-playback operates on the same principle as the magnetic tape recorder but uses discs instead of tape. Each disc must be recorded individually, so the system is not suited to mass production. It is, however, an excellent device for practice use in language laboratories, since the record may be erased or started at a midway point without any rewinding which would be needed with a tape recorder.

Tape Recordings

Practically speaking, most classroom magnetic recording and playback is of the monophonic audio type. High quality monophonic music is acceptable for most classroom use. Other magnetic recording devices, such as video tape and audio wire, are either too new or too old to justify their inclusion in this handbook of practical teaching tools.

Recording Tape. Modern tape for audio recording is a thin, flexible plastic ribbon, ¼ inch wide, coated on one side with iron oxide. The microscopic oxide particles can be magnetized, and it is this fact that permits a "magnetic picture" of sound to be recorded—and reproduced—at will.

Early tapes were made of kraft paper, but the two most common base materials today are cellulose acetate and polyester. Acetate tape is smooth, flexible, and inexpensive. However, when subjected to a sharp pull, it may break. Polyester tape is endowed with similar smooth-

Fig. 6.4—Modern tape recorders are easy enough for even a pupil to use. The student soon discovers for himself the shortcomings of his own speech. (A. Winegarden)

ness and flexibility, but at slightly greater cost. Though polyester tape is very difficult to break, it will stretch—especially the thinner, long playing varieties. Since sound distortion will result from a stretched tape, excessive tension should be avoided.

Oxide color. The color oxide on the tape you use will often indicate its recording characteristics. Standard, all purpose tape usually has a reddish brown oxide. A green coating indicates that the tape will give a high audio output, and a dark red oxide shows it was designed for high quality sound reproduction. Since different oxides have various purposes, you should know the type of material you intend to record, and select a tape oxide accordingly.

Tape Size. There are three standard thicknesses for audio recording tape: 1½ mil, 1 mil, and ½ mil. (Note: a "mil" or "mill" is 1/1,000 of an inch, not 1 millimeter.) It follows, therefore, that the thinner the tape is, the greater the quantity which will fit on a reel of any given size. Standard reel sizes are measured in diameter—3″, 5″, and 7″. Larger reels are available for use on professional studio equipment.

The 3″ reel is used largely in miniature equipment and as an "audio letter." Five and seven inch reels are standard for both home and school use, since they can hold enough recording time for both average situations.

Tape Speed. The amount of tape which passes the recording or playback "head" in one second is known as the tape speed. Professional equipment uses a rate of 30 or 15 inches per second. These are seldom used on school-type machines. Most often, your machine will have two speeds, 7½ i.p.s. and 3¾ i.p.s. Slower speeds are available too, but they often result in a sacrifice of recording quality in return for increased recording time. They are 1⅞ and $^{15}/_{16}$ i.p.s.

The 7½ inch rate is adequate for most speech and music reproduction. For most conversational use, the 3¾ speed will suffice, though 7½ should be preferred if length of recording time is not a factor.

How It Works. A tape recorder is a device which draws a ribbon of oxide coated tape from a feed reel, past an erase head and a record-playback head, to a takeup reel.

Fig. 6.5—Most tape recorders use a recording and drive system as shown here. The drive capstan draws the tape from a supply reel, past an erase head and a record/ playback head, onto a takeup reel.

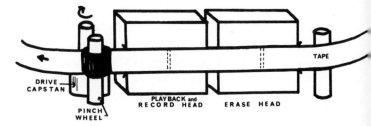

The basic tape transport mechanism, or deck, should be capable of at least 2 speeds (preferably 7½ i.p.s. and 3¾ i.p.s.) and should have a digital elapsed tape indicator (usually a rotating number counter), rapid tape rewind, excellent braking, simple, easy to read functional controls. Reel hubs should be balanced to prevent sound distortion.

Tape is usually provided by a motor driven capstan rather than by a driven takeup reel. This is necessary to insure constant speed past the recording head.

The electronic system of the tape recorder must be capable of erasing a tape, of recording on it, and of playback.

Since most tape recorders erase the previously recorded track immediately prior to recording, there must be a foolproof method of setting the machine into recording position. It must demand an intelligent action, lest a tape be erased by the thoughtless pushing of a "record" button, when all you wanted to do was *play* the tape. Most machines accomplish this by making recording a two handed or difficult motion— so that you don't forget that you're about to record.

Input to a tape recorder may be by microphone, or directly from a radio, phonograph, or other audio device.

The correct level of input is best determined by a meter, which is found on all better recorders, or by an electronic "tuning eye." Over-recording causes a distorted, mushy sound, whereas under-recording requires extreme amplification to make the tape usable—and results in excessive background noise.

During recording, a valuable device to have is the pause control, which permits you to stop the tape without having to change the "record" or "listen" function switch from the position being used.

Output should be of at least three types:

1. *Monitor* which permits you to listen with headphones to the exact sound being recorded.
2. *Internal Speaker*.
3. *External Speaker* jack, for connection of extra, more distant loudspeakers.

How Many Tracks? Tape recorders originally used the full ¼″ tape width to record sound. This system is called *single track* (or full track) recording. It is still the system under which tapes are recorded for schools by the National Tape Depository (DAVI-NEA). It is the system which *must* be used for any tape that may later be edited by splicing.

In order to put more recording time on a given length of tape, audio engineers developed a *dual track* recording-playback head, which records

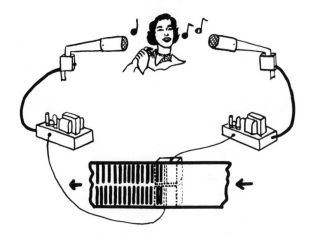

Fig. 6.6—Stereophonic recording uses separate tracks on magnetic tape to reproduce the sound from each amplifier channel.

on only ½ the tape width in each direction of travel. For example, when the tape travels from left to right, it may record only on the bottom half. When all the tape is on the right reel, the operator changes the direction switch and the recorder uses the top half of the tape during the right to left motion.

Of course, if two tracks could be recorded simultaneously, *stereophonic* sound could be (and was) developed. In the stereo system two separate recording channels are used to power two individual recording heads. Thus, the tape has on it sound "picked up" by microphones at two different locations. When these two separate tracks are simultaneously played back into two loudspeakers spaced apart, as the original microphones were, the listener gets a "live" effect. Stereo playback may be valuable for music appreciation of prerecorded commercial tapes, but its application in the classroom is limited.

Naturally, when engineers developed two tracks, they had the natural inclination to try for four. And they did. This means that twice the stereo time, or greater stereo effect, or 4x the monophonic time can be recorded on each tape.

While single track recording is preferred for classroom use, this does not imply that your recorder must be only a single track full width device. Even though your machine may be able to record four tracks, you'll be safe for future editing by merely recording one track and stopping there. Then you can still have the advantage of playing pre-recorded stereo tapes while retaining the ease of editing a single track tape.

Special Purpose Recorders. Although most teachers will use standard tape recorders, certain types are valuable for special purposes.

Some machines are pre-recorded with a certain lesson of a given length. Thereafter they will repeat the same message either continuously or a pre-set number of times.

Another recorder used in speech work permits a student to record a short passage, push a button, and have his voice immediately played back.

In remedial language work, still another kind allows a pupil to place a special tape-striped card in the recorder. The card may contain a word-sound, picture-sound, or all three. Both teacher and pupil may record on the card.

Cartridge loading recorders simplify operation, but they limit you to tapes in compatible cartridges.

Innumerable recorder variations are available for language laboratory use.

How To Do It in Sound

Recording Without a Microphone. Want to record a radio program, a borrowed phonograph record, or another tape? You plug a microphone into your tape recorder, hold it next to the loudspeaker of the radio, phonograph, or tape recorder, and record.

Unfortunately, that's the way most people would do it; and, in so doing, they cut their possible recording quality in half! The recording microphone supplied with the average tape recorder is capable of reproducing well a maximum of about an 8,000 cycle tone; the average small loudspeaker even less. Also, extraneous sounds and background noises can't be avoided when you use a microphone!

The best way to improve sound quality is to eliminate both microphone and loudspeaker, the factors which tend to reduce quality.

If the radio, phonograph, or recorder, whose output you wish to duplicate, has a high impedance output jack (often labelled "auxiliary amplifier output"), merely connect the output patch cord to a high impedance tape recorder input (marked phono/radio). The same is true of matched low impedance output and input, but low impedance inputs are seldom found on non-professional recorders.

In cases where there is no high impedance output jack on a radio, recorder, or phonograph, your local radio repairman can easily install one for $5-$10.

Or, you can purchase a recorder patch cord for under $1. To use it, merely attach the clips on one end of the shielded cord to the voice coil terminals of a speaker and plug the other end into a tape recorder. This is the least desirable of the direct wired methods of recording, since there is usually a severe impedance mismatch between the voice coil of the loudspeaker and the recorder input. This mismatch results in a loss of frequency response. The condition can be corrected by adding to the

Fig. 6.7—A first grade pupil uses the Language Master® for word recognition. He can see the word while he hears it, and can play the card over and over. The device works well with picture/sound identification too. (*Bell & Howell*)

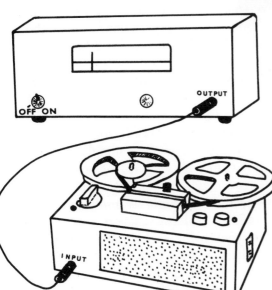

Fig. 6.8—Recording from an audio device such as a record player, radio, or tape recorder, is best done by the direct method using a patch cord from the output jack to the recorder input.

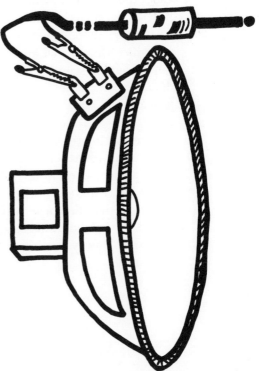

Fig. 6.9—If your phonograph, tape recorder, or radio does not have an output jack, but the voice coil terminals of the device's loudspeaker are easily accessible, you can often make a good quality recording by using a special patch cord of the type shown. The two clips are attached to the two voice coil terminals on most loudspeakers and the jack is then plugged into the recorder's input.

patch cord an in-line audio matching transformer. If you're handy with soldering iron and wire-cutters, you can do the job yourself. If not, see your local radio repairman.

The output of a phonograph crystal or ceramic cartridge is usually electrically suitable for direct connection to a tape recorder input jack.

When you copy a tape, you can also change recording speed. A tape originally recorded at 7½" i.p.s. could be "dubbed" (or copied) at a slower speed, say 3¾ or 1⅞. However when you "dub" at a speed different from that of the original recording, poorer quality may result. Make a test recording first to see if you are satisfied with the quality of the copy before you do the whole tape.

Record It Live! Not all tape recording is done by direct patch from another piece of electronic equipment. You may want to record a lesson, dramatic presentation, or other live sound yourself. It would be foolish to pretend that the task is simple. But, as long as you don't expect the precise timing and effects of the professional, you can do a creditable job of local live recording.

The best recording is accomplished in a studio with a separate control booth. All live sounds to be recorded take place in the soundproofed studio and are fed by microphone cables to the control room, where the actual equipment operation takes place. Truly, this is ideal; for all extraneous sounds are isolated from the microphones. Sounds such as the motor noise of the tape recorder, switch clicks, airplanes overhead, passing autos—all are so familiar that we may not even notice them—but the tape recorder will. Thus the recording studio is preferred, but practically speaking, it won't be available to most teachers.

How, then, can you record in your own classroom? On the assumption that a classroom has pupils, the first step is to train those pupils not to wiggle! Once they hear the devastating results of *their* definition of "quiet," a most important hurdle is spanned. To do this, just ask the class to be as quiet as they possibly can, for one minute. Then turn the recording level of your tape recorder up to maximum, and record merely the ambient "quiet" for the minute. The playback results will amaze you as well as your class. The fantastic amount of noise present even in a "quiet" classroom should shock your pupils into a real effort at being silent during recording. (Some pupils may recognize that the "demonstration" took place with a "stacked deck"—never would you record at maximum gain in any standard dramatic production or lesson. How you answer that query will be public testimony to your ingenuity!)

Once the "silent class" is established, what can you do with other noises. Closed windows and doors will reduce some sounds, but other sounds cannot be lessened substantially. If the non-reducible sounds are infrequent, the answer is don't tape during such periods. Just push the pause control and stop the tape. You can always continue live recording where you paused; but you can't later eliminate, for example, an airplane sound which is superimposed on your dramatic production or lesson. You might even assign one pupil the function of "listener," who informs the producer by hand signal as soon as he detects an approaching extraneous sound.

The easiest recording to make is that of a single voice. One person can operate the recorder, monitor with headphones and direct the speaker during the recording. The only problem involved is maintaining proper recording level. This is done by the recorder operator who monitors the sound being taped and adjusts it for proper level. The narrator should be approximately 12" from the microphone, and should keep the same distance and direction from it throughout the recording session.

Microphones supplied with tape recorders seldom have cords over 8 feet long, and the cord can't be lengthened with extensions unless you're willing to sacrifice sound quality. With the microphone so close to the recorder, it can easily pick up motor and switch sounds. The best way to cure this problem is to use the microphone's own directional characteristics. A unidirectional microphone, placed so that its pickup pattern is away from the recorder, can suppress the recording of extraneous sounds to such an extent that it may be no longer objectionable.

Background effects can be added by record. Musical background is easiest to do. It involves merely operating a phonograph near the microphone pickup. Variation in music level (e.g. "up" during the narrator's pauses, and "under" or "out" during narration) is handled by the pupil operating the phonograph by a mere twist of the phonograph volume control. The recorder operator or producer—whichever one has the duty of headphone monitoring—directs the phonograph operator as well as the narrator.

Live sound effects are usually handled on a separate microphone. Since there is generally only one microphone input, a dual input adapter is necessary. The adapter is equipped with volume controls to pre-balance the relative level of speech to sound effects—as desired by the director—, for the recorder operator generally has only one control to vary amplification of the input.

If you wish to vary multiple microphone inputs simultaneously—

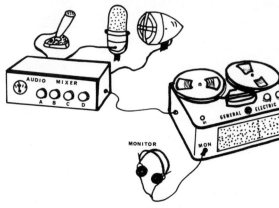

Fig. 6.10—Dual Input
Adapter. (*Bell & Howell*)

Fig. 6.11—Sound input from multiple microphones
is converted by the audio mixer into one electrical
signal for input to the recorder. An audio mixer
lets you balance inputs so that the proper effect
is heard on the monitor headphones, and recorded on the tape.

as would be done in an actual broadcast recording session—another electronic device is needed—the audio mixer. It permits multiple mike inputs with individual control and no loss of quality.

A few other hints to the beginning producer are in order. During
a recording session, you should station a monitor at the door to your
classroom to prevent unauthorized entry. Instruct all speakers to handle
scripts without crinkling paper. This takes a little practice. Agree on
silent hand signals with which to direct actors, since voice directions are
impossible. A visit to a radio studio during a live dramatic recording
session would be an invaluable prelude to your own classroom tape
project.

Tape Care. Proper tape care requires your attention in four basic
areas: cleaning, demagnetization precautions, handling, and storage.

Cleaning. The parts touched by the tape rather than the tape itself
must generally be cleaned. The recording-erase heads, drive capstan, and
tape guides are constantly in contact with tape, and magnetic oxides are
worn from the tape. The best advice on cleaning is to follow the directions in the recorder's instruction book. But, since instruction books are
notorious for their ability to disappear, here are a few suggestions.

A special head cleaner solution should be purchased from an electronics parts dealer. The bottle usually has an applicator cap, but a cotton swab or camel hair brush may be used. If you don't want to go through
all this, you can merely use a cleaning tape. This novel item threads into
the machine and is run in the usual way. In so doing, it passes over all

112

the parts which the recording tape touches and it cleans them. Cleaning tape also lubricates the path and heads with a silicone lubricant that lessens friction.

Although tape cleaning is generally unnecessary, you might need to do it if your tapes have gotten particularly dusty. Although tape can be cleaned by merely holding a clean, dry, lint-free cloth against the oxide coated side of the tape during rewind, you'll be better off if you use a special tape cleaning cloth which not only cleans, but lubricates.

Demagnetization. The bulk tape eraser, which is a powerful electromagnet, is used to erase an entire reel of tape instantly. Since a strong magnetic field can erase recording tape, it follows that tape should never be near one. Such fields could exist near powerful motors or magnetic devices which produce action, such as relays and electromagnets. While accidental erasure is possible, it is unlikely. Nevertheless, the ounce of prevention is well worth using.

Handling. When we speak of handling recording tape, we seldom mean by people. Rather, it is the machine which does the handling. Some recorders subject tape to excessive tension during winding. This happens in two ways: first, by an excessive stress on the tape causing it to elongate, and second, by the tremendous pressure on the tape nearest the hub after a tape has been wound too tightly. The only cure for such poor handling is to have the machine professionally serviced to lessen tension.

Storage. Temperature and humidity, in addition to storage away from heavy magnetic fields, are factors which should be considered. Acetate tapes become brittle after prolonged low humidity storage. High temperature causes loss of strength and dimensional tape distortion. Polyester tape is relatively unaffected by humidity in short term storage, but it is affected by extremes of temperature. If tape must be stored or shipped under extreme temperatures, allow about 20 hours for it to return to room temperature before using. Occasional use helps to keep tape in good condition by releasing internal strains which might be present.

For long storage (five years or more) keep acetate tape in a sealed container. Polyester tapes are best kept unsealed unless the interior of the container can be kept extremely dry.

How to Splice. Either because you wish to edit out some portion of tape, or because of tape breakage, any teacher who uses the tape recorder must know how to splice. In fact, a roll of splicing tape and a splicing block are as indispensable as the recording tape itself. Tape splicing is easy. Just follow these five simple steps, which are shown in the accompanying illustrations. *Always use special splicing tape* (such as "Scotch"® No. 41).

1. Hold overlapped ends of magnetic tape securely between fingers and cut at shallow angle—about 45 degrees—for maximum strength and flexibility of splice.

2. Butt the cut ends of the tape in a splicing block without overlapping them. Make sure you apply the splicing tape to the shiny side of the magnetic tape.

3. Apply small section of splicing tape. Use the $\frac{7}{32}''$ size and apply it parallel with the magnetic tape as shown. Rub splicing tape firmly with fingernail to iron out air pockets for positive adhesion.

4. If a splicing block is not available, lay magnetic tape on a flat surface. Butt the cut edges carefully and hold in position with index and forefinger. Apply short strip of $\frac{1}{2}''$ or $\frac{3}{4}''$ wide splicing tape diagonally across splice and rub firmly to remove all air pockets.

5. If splicing tape is wider than the magnetic tape used, trim off excess, cutting into magnetic tape very slightly. This eliminates danger of exposed adhesive gumming up recording head or sticking to adjacent layer of magnetic tape.

After you become an expert at splicing, you might want to splice in special tapes. Leader timer tape has 1 second markings at standard speeds, and colored tapes are available to help identify the location of certain selections on a tape reel.

Edit Your Tape. The first tapes you make yourself will probably be straight recording. But it won't take long for you to critically assay certain parts, and wish that they could be removed. When you reach that stage, you're ready to edit. You may even want to remove a single word. Or you may want to put in some material from another tape. Whatever the reason, editing is easy enough to perform if you're willing to practice a little. These steps show the basic editing technique you'll need:

1. Listen to your recorded tape and list the parts to be edited. A tape index on your recorder is invaluable for this purpose.
2. Replay the tape and stop at the first point to be edited. To find the exact spot to cut, move the tape manually across the head with the machine in playback position.
3. Mark cutting points with a grease pencil or with a fine felt marking pen on the shiny side of the tape.
4. Cut the tape (see "How to Splice," above) at the exact editing point and remove marks if you used a grease pencil. Splice.
5. Go on to the next editing point and repeat the procedure.

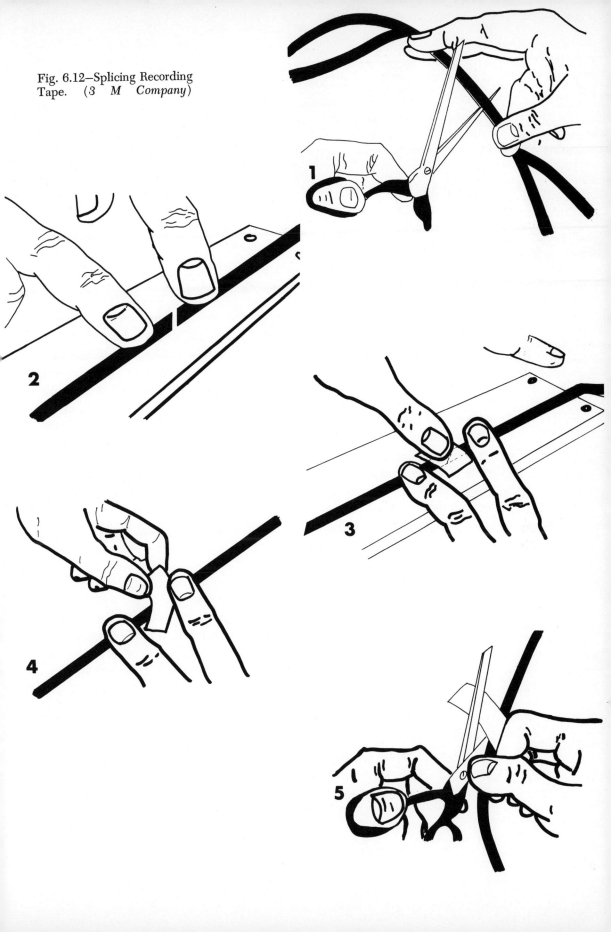

Fig. 6.12—Splicing Recording
Tape. (*3   M   Company*)

Fig. 6.13—This first grader listens intently to a story and reads it at the same time in the Listening Corner of a classroom.

Sound in Your Classroom

Whether it's on disc or tape, recorded sound is an exciting addition to education. Since both serve the same purpose—though by a different means—the use suggestions which follow might be applicable to both devices.

Speech. In speech correction, the tape recorder is vital. Certainly recognition of a problem is the first step in its cure. By recording pupils' voices, they can be encouraged to locate their own defects and work on appropriate remedial action under teacher guidance. With specialized tape recording equipment, speech students can record a word or phrase after hearing it on tape, and then receive an instantaneous playback by merely pushing a button. Discs can be used individually, too, as examples of acceptable speech.

The Listening Corner.[1] "Have you ever tried using recorded materials with a few pupils while the rest of the class—undistracted—is busily occupied preparing a language lesson?

"Impossible!" you say.

Not at all.

In a classroom "Listening Corner," a pupil may participate in educational listening activities entirely without distraction to his classmates. The key to the Listening Corner's success lies in the use of headphones rather than loudspeakers for the production of sound. This provides an unusual type of individuality, for in using headphones, extraneous classroom sounds are effectively eliminated. All that the pupil hears is the audio material on which he is concentrating. By this method, a psychological unity, difficult to obtain on non-headphone listening, is established between the listener and the audio material being presented.

---

[1] Adapted from Herbert E. Scuorzo, "The Listening Corner," *Grade Teacher,* Teachers Publishing Corp., March, 1962, pp. 54-55.

Only a teacher-single pupil relationship could provide more individualized instruction.

A wide variety of materials is available for use in a classroom Listening Corner.

One of the most interesting is the *Audio Book,* a full length or abridged version of a standard classic, recorded by a professional actor or reader, on a 16⅔ rpm seven-inch disc. Because of the slow recording speed, up to one hour of recording time may be found on a single disc. In using the *Audio Book,* children do not have to depend solely on their own ability to interpret the words of the author correctly. They may hear those same words read, with expert emphasis, by professional actors and actresses. Since much of our literature was intended to be spoken, *Audio Book* listening may satisfy that need.

Offerings include such titles as *Alice in Wonderland, Treasure Island, The Call of the Wild, The Just So Stories* and many other works suitable for elementary school use.

Also necessary in the complete Listening Corner are dramatization recordings. While dramatizations are available in most literature areas covered by the *Audio Books,* their most effective use has been in the social studies. An outstanding example of the social studies dramatizations is found in the *Landmarks of America* series. Included are many important events—for example *The Panama Canal, California Gold Rush, The Louisiana Purchase* and *The Erie Canal.* Enrichment Records which are based on *Landmark Books* are available and correlate with enrichment filmstrips on the same subjects.

Excellent results have been achieved by using all three materials—filmstrip, book, and records with independent pupil teams. A culminating group discussion may be conducted to provide total class participation in the experiences of each group. Here, too, the record team should use the classroom Listening Corner, since the recorded sound would not then be audible to the other committees.

Individual enrichment is also possible through the use of the documentary recordings. One of the best known documentary series is the *I Can Hear It Now* folio. Through the medium of records the pupil may experience the thrill of hearing the actual voices of men who have made recent history.

Another unusual approach to instruction through recordings is found in the *Musical Multiplication Tables.* With his multiplication facts set to music the pupil should be able to master them individually as simply as he could learn a popular tune. While the principle of learning facts by setting them to music is not new, the use of these recordings in the classroom on an individual basis would provide the interesting variant.

The sound filmstrip (a filmstrip and a recording) also presents interesting possibilities for Listening Corner use. With simple instruction in the operation of the filmstrip viewer and the filmstrip-record pacing system, most upper elementary pupils would be able to operate the equipment. Used in the Listening Corner as a supplementary enrichment device, the sound filmstrip has few competitors for the pupil not only sees and hears individually but also may repeat portions of the filmstrip and record if he finds it necessary.

Audio Books, enrichment dramatizations, documentaries and sound filmstrips are some of the variety of disc recordings which have been successfully used by pupils in the Listening Corner.

While not as widely used in classrooms as disc recordings, tape recordings show a tremendous potential for the future. Unlimited opportunity is presented for the use of locally prepared recordings. In addition, teachers throughout the nation have easy access to 6,500 tapes on a wide range of topics, for use in kindergarten through adult education, from the National Tape Repository. An informative leaflet about the Repository may be secured on request from the Department of Audio Visual Instruction (NEA).

The Listening Corner should contain, as basic equipment, a standard school model 4 speed phonograph with a headphone jack, headphone sets, a headphone junction box and a tape recorder. As you put your Listening Corner into use, you will undoubtedly find that you could make good use of a television set and a radio. If possible, inclusion of these items should be considered also. You could begin a Listening Corner in your class with only a phonograph and a few recordings. Why not try it? You can make it a significant teaching aid for you, and a valuable learning device for your pupils."

Introducing the Tape Recorder. A good way to introduce pupils to the recorder is to have them listen. Secure a dramatic tape from your local tape library or, at a nominal fee, have a story recorded on your own tape by the National Tape Recording Service—a project sponsored by the National Education Association's Department of Audiovisual Instruction, the National Association of Broadcasters, and the University of Colorado. (Write NEA, 1201 16th Street, N. W., Washington 6, D.C., for a catalog, $1.50.)

Let your pupils listen to the tape. Later, ask them how they would like to record selections of their own. Begin with short anecdotes written by each pupil as a language lesson. The anecdotes may then be recorded and students can listen to their own voices presenting the works they composed.

Dramatic Use of Tape. For dramatic presentations, the tape recorder has no peer. Pupils gain new insight into the world of radio dramatics by acting in a recorded play themselves. While original productions are certainly desirable from a creative standpoint, the insight, impact, and feeling gained from producing a professionally-written radio play is of immense value in stimulating true creativity. In a recorded dramatization, much of the "live" feeling is simulated. The absence of visual content leaves the voice and sound effects as sole carriers of the message. Actors selected for a recorded presentation should be chosen on the basis of recorded performance, not live tryouts. You may find that different stars will shine—and that alone is a desirable outcome.

Use Records and Tape in Language Arts. Want to do some memorization or choral speaking? Record your own voice, as leader, and let the class follow. You'll be able to give more attention to the difficulties encountered by individual pupils.

Have you ever used paced dictation? It can serve to improve pupils' spelling, punctuation, and understanding of sentence structure. Tape your properly timed dictation in advance. You'll find it time well spent.

At a more advanced level, pupils can be made to improve storytelling techniques, emphasis, and other characteristics if they can hear themselves on tape.

Your pupils can exchange tapes with children in other lands. This will provide a language experience and social studies experience as well.

Tape recorded children's books have been found to be helpful, at primary grade levels, in reading instruction. The tape gives the text orally, while the pupil sees the printed version. Using headsets in a listening corner technique, a pupil may listen and read without disturbing his classmates. This system has been particularly useful in helping students relate the printed word to the flow of speech.

In some cases, a tape recorder can be used to help pupils at all levels achieve better word recognition skill. The Language Master® lets pupils work independently in achieving better language facility. You can make your own tape cards or buy them ready-made.

When teaching children whose native tongue is not English this tape recorder is an invaluable tool for allowing the student to hear specific words or phrases, and to practice and hear his own repetition.

Social Studies needs Sound. The world of discs is an amazing treasure for the social studies class. Voices of famous men and women and actual events of history are available through the ubiquitous disc. A library of recordings in the social sciences should be available in your listening corner.

If you've produced some films locally for your social studies program, you may want to add some sound.

While projecting the picture, record whatever narrative or musical sound track you wish on your tape recorder. Since synchronization will not be exact, always develop your narrative so that it does not depend directly on the sequence being projected. If you must speak directly about a picture on the screen, make certain to stop speaking about it a few seconds before that sequence ends. In this way, you'll have some leeway.

Sound slide shows, too, can be developed by coordinating a taped sound track with 2 x 2 slides.

Committee Reports can be made on tape. Then your students can listen to their own oral presentation with an eye toward improvement. This is an especially valuable technique for field trip reports. A portable, battery operated recorder taken on a field trip, can be used to record on-site voices and sounds for replay to other pupils.

Music on Tape and Disc. Disc recordings of musical selections are so commonplace that you need not be introduced to them. But how should they be used. If the only use is "enjoyment" listening, the student can do that at home. But true enjoyment goes deeper, and the teacher should develop real appreciation of all kinds of music through its sound characteristics, mood, history, development and other factors that created it. Music can be the spark to cause spontaneous art activity, or to interest students in "strange sounds" created by foreign native instruments. Whatever your musical goal, the chances are good that disc recordings will help you to achieve it.

Remember, discs are easily damaged or scratched. If a particular record is to be used repeatedly, tape it and file the original disc away.

Assembly programs often need musical accompaniment or sound effects. You can provide both with a tape recorder by recording them in advance and playing them back at the right time. Recorded music and sound effects have certain advantages over "live" ones; recorded sound can be amplified to compensate for the absorption that takes place in any crowded auditorium, and also, there is no chance of error, since you've selected only the best tape presentation to use during the actual program.

Taping the music for your class play or graduation exercises allows for practice sessions to be held even when the accompanist is not available.

School orchestra and chorus practice sessions should be taped to allow the members to gain an appreciation of the total sound. Individual and group performers can also benefit from hearing themselves.

Evaluation and Supplemental Use of Tapes. The audio quiz is another novel tape recorder application. Pupils are asked to identify musical selections, famous quotations, sounds of instruments, or any other element where learning depends on sound.

Pupils who are absent can make up oral assignments on tape and you can listen to it at your convenience.

Students who are confined due to illness can have the benefit of class discussion via tapes sent to them daily. It's extremely economical since tapes can be used over and over.

Fig. 6.14—This first page of *Sound and Musical Instruments,* by E. Tristram and Jack Barrows (edited by A. Fraleigh), a science tape script shows how an actual classroom lesson can be put on tape in a manner that demands pupil activity and involvement. (Norwalk, Conn. Board of Education)

Prepared by Elinor Tristram

Time: 20 min.

Edited by Alton Fraleigh
Art Work by John A. Barrows
Enrichment to Science Unit on Sound

▼ = Indicates music
to be played

Copyright Norwalk Board of Education, 1964

SOUND AND MUSICAL INSTRUMENTS

-Elinor Tristram, Jefferson
Grades 3, 4, 5

Introduction - (Opens with music)

In our listening tape today, children, we are going to try to discover three characteristics of all sounds. Tune your ears for good listening and enjoy yourselves.

Music is an art, the art of expressing ideas and feelings through musical sounds. Music, at the same time, is a science, the science of sound. Music is sound put to certain rhythm or time. There are many kinds of sounds. Today, boys and girls, we will discover how musical instruments make different sounds.

First, let us listen to a tone on the piano. ▼ Does it sound "high" or "low"? At No. 1, circle the correct word on your worksheet. Listen again to a different tone on the piano. ▼ Was it "high" or "low"? At No. 2, circle the correct word.

Now listen to a tone on a different instrument - the bells ▼ (a high tone). At No. 3, circle "high" or "low". Listen to this tone ▼ (a low tone). At No. 4, circle high or low.

From these two examples, what have you discovered sound has? The high or low sound, children, is called pitch, p - i - t - c - h. At Roman Numeral I, write the first characteristic of all sound.

Important addresses at professional meetings can be taped and played back for teachers who were unable to attend.

Radio broadcasts can be taped for later use at a time that is more suitable for instruction.

Tape Your Lesson. Most classroom use of tape is supplementary. It need not be.

Complete science lessons have been produced on tape by Georgian Court College, Lakewood, N.J.

The Norwalk, Connecticut, Board of Education has established an extensive program involving direct teaching by tape.

The Future of Recordings in School. Both discs and tapes are established as teaching tools. The dream of the future is here, and only the cost barrier remains to be broken.

Both picture and sound can be recorded on either tape or disc. Future costs may well be low enough to let the classroom TV screen, backed by audio-visual discs or tapes, take on the role of the *only* needed AV device.

Chapter Seven

CHALK
AND DISPLAY BOARDS

From the days of stick drawing in the sand, teachers have communicated visually with pupils. Most of the time, such communication can and will be planned in advance. But there comes the time when a need arises for an unforeseen visual. What should you use? The first device which comes to mind is the chalkboard.

The Chalkboard

Some teachers treat the chalkboard as an upright drawing board, and write everything with the care and deliberation of a draftsman. Others regard it as a mere extension of a sheet of scrap paper—and their "chicken tracks" across it are generally illegible to their pupils. Between these two extremes lies reasonable classroom use.

If the former is your goal—why not use an overhead transparency instead. You'll be able to do all the instantaneous writing you want, and still have your draftsman-like diagram. Only it will be permanent. You can file it away for future use, not having to give any thought to the beautiful drawing you'd have to erase from the chalkboard sooner or later. It's obvious then, that using the chalkboard for the display of precision maps or drawings—which may be difficult to prepare—is a needless time waster.

The other misuse of the media, careless scribble, is even worse, for it wastes your students' time too! The teacher who constantly holds a piece of chalk, and is forever writing may be doing wonders for his own security by avoiding face to face contact with his pupils, but he's not doing much instruction!

The chalkboard is *a* tool, but not the only tool, through which a good teacher can communicate with his pupils. *When it will best handle the task,* use it!

What the Chalkboard Can Do. Like any tool, there are specific areas where chalkboard use is indicated:

Lost in Space. Have you ever had the feeling that you're trying to teach a brick wall. You talk, everyone listens, but few seem to "hear." That blank, vacant stare greets you from a score of once shining, bright eyed understanding faces. Certainly you planned your instruction, but you didn't expect *this* reaction. Now is the time for you to reduce your abstract verbiage to simple chalkboard visuals.

Or possibly you've just used one method of communication—lecture, or discussion, or some other—a bit too long. Variation is needed, and the chalkboard is ready. Change of media can be a valuable technique in keeping pupil interest level high.

Pupil Participation. Organized pupil participation in a lesson involving the chalkboard is another way for creating interest. Most children love to contribute to the class if it involves writing on the chalkboard. You'll never want for volunteers if you've organized, for example, a map study lesson in which pupils insert product symbols. The few who fail to participate might have had poor experiences due to chalkboard misuse, but they can generally be removed from the anti-chalkboard league, if you make certain that such students will meet with success.

The type of situation to be avoided is having the mass going to the board "to write your arithmetic homework." This kind of assignment violates two basic concepts of reasonableness. The material written on a chalkboard for all to see should be correct. It should be placed there under the constant eye of the teacher, and incorrect matter should be immediately corrected. This is obviously impossible to do if you allow 6 or 10 children each to place an arithmetic problem on the chalkboard simultaneously. Secondly, it defeats one of the prime advantages of the chalkboard as an attention getter. If numerous children write on the board, you'll have to fight to get students' eyes from gazing at problems other than the one under instruction.

Make Your Own Chalkboard (*or cover it up*). With chalkboard, it's generally either feast or famine. If yours is a classroom with wall-to-wall and ceiling to floor chalkboard, you're more interested in covering it up—usually for "some bulletin board space." Of course, your best solution is to request that a bulletin board be installed in place of one of the excess chalkboards. Failing that, all you need is a few dollars and permission to place some ½″ thick wood fiber wallboard sheets (available from your local lumber dealer) over the chalkboard and tack it to the wooden mouldings. Or, for permanence, you could even attach it to the face of a *slate blackboard* with a water base linoleum paste. (Don't use a waterproof paste, for some day, another teacher may want to remove it, and waterproof paste presents an immense task.)

Increasing your chalkboard area is just as easy. Ask for one, and failing that, request permission to install your own. Small chalkboards can easily be made from a sheet of tempered hardboard (Masonite®) which you paint with a composition chalkboard paint (available from your local school supplier or direct from Beckley Cardy Co., Chicago, Ill.). This surface will not even approach the wearing quality of a standard slate, glass, porcelain, or plastic laminate chalkboard, but it will provide a serviceable emergency writing surface.

Pounce Patterns.[1] You are standing at the chalkboard—a small map in one hand, a piece of chalk in the other. A glance at the map—a short chalk line is drawn. Another glance, another line segment. Again. And again. No, that wasn't right. Erase, smudge, try again, There! You're finished! You step back to view—and exasperation sets in. It just doesn't *look* like South America!

To most teachers, this experience is a common one. The problem of how to draw an accurate outline map on the chalkboard is one of long standing. While under most conditions there is little reason for using patterns, technical accuracy is essential in map making.

The pounce pattern, while ideally suited to outline map making, could serve equally well in any application where an accurate outline must be transferred to the chalkboard.

Pounce patterns are easy to make, a pleasure to use, and simple to store for future use.

Your pupils will enjoy making and using the pounce pattern, too. Just have them follow these simple steps.

1. Draw the desired outline map on sheet of heavy kraft wrapping paper. A hard, tough paper will serve better than a soft one. The map must be drawn the same size you wish to have it on your chalkboard.

2. Place the completed outline drawing over a piece of soft fiber ceiling tile. Be certain that the flat or untextured side is facing up. Although the use of a fiber tile is preferred, a sturdy corrugated board may be substituted. Punch holes along the entire outline at about half-

---

[1] H. E. Scuorzo, "Pounce Patterns," *Grade Teacher,* Teachers Publishing Corp., November 1961, pp. 34-35.

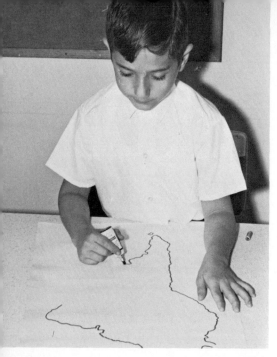

Fig. 7.1A—Making
a Pounce Pattern.

Fig. 7.1B

inch intervals with an awl (the steel point of a pencil compass will serve also). Each hole should be about $\frac{1}{16}$ to $\frac{1}{8}$ inch in diameter. The portion of the outline *must* be over some part of the fiber tile. Inspect to see that the holes have been punched "clean."

3. Attach the completely punched outline map to a clean chalkboard with masking tape, magnets or in some other temporary manner. Pounce a dusty eraser over all of the punched holes on the outline. Wherever there is a hole in the paper, chalk dust will settle on the chalkboard. Next, remove the pattern and store it for future use.

4. Small dots will be visible on the chalkboard wherever there were holes in the pattern. Merely connect the dots, and your outline map is ready for use.

Stage a dramatic effect by connecting the dots while the pupils look on from their seats. The tiny dots, readily visible to you will be invisible to them. The class will be amazed at your new-found cartographic ability!

Enlarging Squares. Even if your drawing ability is quite limited, you can successfully convert a small line drawing original to a chalkboard enlargement, though projection equipment isn't available to do the enlarging for you.

If you want to permanently square the chalkboard, you can inscribe squares into the chalkboard surface with a scribing tool. However, this method is generally not recommended, since the size of the

126

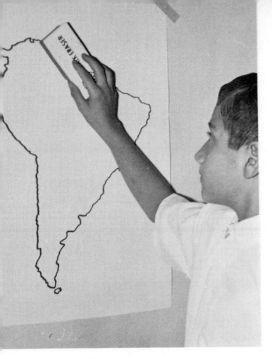

Fig. 7.1C

Fig. 7.1D

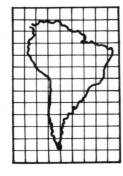

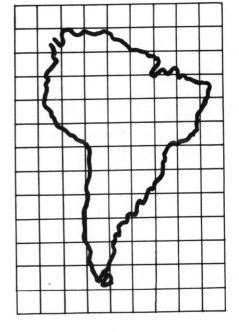

Fig. 7.2—Proportionate enlarging of line drawings is easily done by the enlarging square method described in the text.

squares cannot be changed, and the lines, themselves, cannot be removed.

A more desirable method would be to make a pounce pattern of squares, and use it to make a lightly squared impression on the chalkboard.

127

Next, draw squares on the picture to be enlarged. (If you don't want to destroy the picture with squares, a sheet of acetate may be squared with acetate ink or a china marking pencil and used as an overlay.)

Naturally, the degree of enlargement will be the ratio of the area of the small squares on the original to the large squares on the chalkboard. Size of the finished drawing may be varied by changing the dimensions of either the original or chalkboard squares. For ease of transfer, however, the ratio of the side of a square on the chalkboard to the side of a square on the original should be no more than 4 to 1. This will give an area enlargement of 16 times the original.

To use enlarging squares, merely draw in each enlarged box whatever appears in the smaller original. You must still do the drawing yourself, but this method makes the task easier by confining the work to be copied to small segments of the original line drawing.

Projection Enlargement. Line drawing originals may be enlarged for chalkboard use by either the opaque or overhead projector.

If you use an opaque projector, the room will have to be in total darkness due to the limited efficiency of the device. But under conditions of total darkness you'll be able to see enough to permit outlining the enlargement in chalk.

Transparencies, whether the overhead type or slides, may also be used for chalkboard enlargements—and complete darkness isn't needed. However, you will have to make the desired illustration into a transparency first. If you wish to transfer a line illustration from a filmstrip, this, too, can be done directly. Just project on the board and outline in chalk.

The Template. If you use a particular outline shape frequently, a template may be useful. It would be suitable for making chalkboard outlines of maps, chemistry apparatus, geometric shapes, and the like. Draw the outline on plywood, hardboard, or heavy chipboard. It may be cut out with a coping saw or, if you used chipboard, a sharp instrument such as utility or X-Acto® knife.

Secure a small block of wood to the center to serve as a hand grip. It can be glued on with white glue, or stapled from the reverse side. If you choose the latter, be certain to tape over the staples to avoid scratching the chalkboard.

Hold the finished template firmly against the chalkboard and outline it in chalk. If your template is large, you'd better have a pupil assist you in holding it during the outlining.

To improve the quality of your template drawings somewhat, bevel the edge of the template which does not touch the chalkboard. It will result in a sharper line.

Guidelines for Chalkboard Writing. Obviously chalkboard work must contain legendary matter. How should you write, in script or print? The answer completely depends on you.

Writing which is illegible is useless, and the best answer to "what to use" is "What do you do more legibly?"

Legibility is by far the most important factor in chalkboard writing. To create legibility your chalkboard writing should have:

1. Well formed letters, properly spaced.
2. Sufficient height, width, and weight.
3. No unusual flourish or shape.
4. Neatness and uniformity.

Vertical writing ability, which is necessary for chalkboard use, is not something one masters at the first attempt. Beginning teachers, since the advent of the chalkboard have been shattering their pupils with "chalk squeak," amusing them with up and down hill writing, and giving them immeasurable moments of pleasure by turning their backs while writing on the chalkboard.

"Well formed letters" does not imply that they must follow "this" form of "standard" writing or "that." It does mean that the letter formation must be such that it is instantly understood by the average reader without any conscious thought whatever. If the reader must stop to think what the letter is—it's not well formed!

Correct minimum letter height is determined by the distance to the farthest student. Everything appears smaller when viewed from a distance, so even your smallest chalkboard lettering must be large enough for all to see. For example, a 4 inch high letter, when viewed from thirty feet away, appears only about 1 inch high.

This means that a 3 to 4 inch high letter is about the smallest which should be used in the average class.

As far as letter weight is concerned, it shouldn't present too much difficulty unless you have a penchant for very fine pointed chalk—and not very many teachers still sharpen their chalk! Amusing as it might seem, sharpened chalk is essential if you're doing detailed drawings. However, consider using some other medium if you must sharpen chalk, for the resultant line would probably be too thin for good viewing and easy writing.

If you want to add to legibility, you should rotate the chalk while writing. This will equalize the width of line somewhat, so that you don't begin the word narrow and clear, and end it with a broad, fuzzy stroke.

If the cardinal sin of chalkboard use isn't talking while writing, then it certainly must be improper use of the pointer. Either one ranks high in the misuse department. When you write on the chalkboard, don't talk. Write first; then teach. And, if you have so much to put on the board that you're afraid you'll waste time, write in advance, or choose some other method of presenting the information. The mimeograph or spirit duplicator does a splendid job of presenting large amounts of text without wasting precious class time.

The other culprit, the pointer, by its nature seems to force teachers to face the chalkboard in order to use it. It need not, and the trick is a simple one. Face the class (while not blocking the chalkboard) at an oblique angle to the board. Hold the pointer in the hand nearest the board. If you're right-handed, stand to the right of the subject matter; if you're left-handed, stand on the left. In this position you can look at class or chalkboard with equal ease.

Colored chalk can serve as an ideal means of accenting chalkboard work. However it can be severely damaging to clothing, so a moist cloth should be used for dustless erasing of color, rather than the standard felt or plastic foam eraser.

Meet the Magnetic Chalkboard.[2] Increasingly throughout the country, magnetic chalkboards are being installed in new and reconditioned classrooms.

The name is somewhat misleading since the chalkboard itself is *not* a magnet. However, due to the board's construction, a strong magnet will adhere to the writing surface, making possible a whole new family of magnetic instructional aids. To find out if your chalkboard is magnetic, just place a strong magnet on its surface. If it holds, you're ready to try magnetic aids.

The number of magnets needed for a particular aid will vary according to the strength of the magnets being used and the weight of the aid to which they are attached. For best results in most situations, a high quality Alnico, ceramic, or plastic magnet should be used.

You can attach alnico or ceramic magnets to aids in a variety of ways. Permanent attachment is achieved by gluing the magnet to the back of the aid. Cellulose household cement will be adequate in most cases.

[2] H. E. Scuorzo, Adapted from "Meet the Magnetic Chalkboard," *Grade Teacher,* Teachers Publishing Corp., September 1961, pp. 44-45 et seq.

Fig. 7.3—The simple outline map on the chalkboard is a product map for this student who places a magnet-backed product illustration in its proper location. Since the products are attached with magnets, removal is simple, and the map may be quickly converted to one showing rainfall, population distribution, cities, or almost anything else.

But magnets are expensive, and most teachers will want to attach their magnets temporarily—being able to remove them easily is a financial saving.

One method of temporary attachment uses a material known to very few teachers. A two-part fabric called Velcro® may be used, one half on the aid, the other half on the magnet. However, since the Velcro system holds rather tightly, a strong adhesive must be used to attach the Velcro parts to the aid and magnet. Otherwise, the Velcro parts may pull loose from aid or magnet, rather than separate from each other.

Another, more conventional, but certainly less imaginative method of temporarily attaching an aid to a magnet is the wood block system. In this method, a soft wood block is glued to a magnet. To attach the aid, merely thumb tack or staple *through* the aid into the wood block.

Flexible plastic magnet strip can be used too, but it is quite expensive. This type of magnet is sold by the foot and can be cut with a scissors. For use in making magnetic aids, you should purchase magnet strip backed with pressure sensitive adhesive.

Excellent magnetic aids are available commercially, but you can make many yourself.

In constructing your own aids, you must consider the stock of which they will be made. The larger the aid is, the heavier the paperboard or tag will have to be. Aids which have thin members (as the upright of a cutout musical note) need heavier stock than those which are on compact shape (as a circle or square).

Here are a few ideas for magnetic aids which may give you some thoughts for your own creations:

Music. Cut out musical notes from at least 10 ply tag stock or 18 point paperboard. With magnets attached to them, the notes can be used on a magnetic chalkboard without erasure. Just line the chalkboard with a staff and move the notes as needed.

131

Fig. 7.4—The magnetic chalkboard isn't limited to static illustrations. This pupil demonstrates to the class his knowledge of directions with a movable compass needle.

Social Studies. Teaching pupils about the school district in which they live? Make a map of the district on thin paper. (You could draw it on the board, but this way the map can be re-used.) Place the map on the magnetic chalkboard with a magnet holding down each corner. The pupil can cut out a magazine illustration which represents his home and glue it to a piece of magnet backed tag stock. Then he can put his own home on the map in its proper place and easily see the location of his school, local stores, and neighbors' homes in relation to each other.

Magnetic aids can move, too. Through the center of a tagboard compass rose place a split rivet. Punch a ¼″ hole in the balance center of a tagboard needle which is slightly longer than the greatest dimension of the rose. Place the needle over the split rivet, then add a washer and spread the rivet apart. Add a magnet to the back and you have a splendid chalkboard compass—all ready for your students to "box." Incidentally, boxing the compass is probably the easiest way to teach pupils basic map reading directions.

You can create some pupil interest in geography with a magnetic product map. Pupils select magazine illustrations of products of an area and glue them to a magnet. Each child can place his own product in the proper location on an outline map you've drawn on the chalkboard.

Arithmetic. Any teacher who has had the experience of trying to juggle fractional parts into position on a flannel board realizes the need for a system which gives greater ease of placement than the flannel board permits. The magnetic board does just that. Fractional parts can be easily adjusted to fit together so that the pupil can develop a kinesthetic approach to fractional understanding.

If your classroom isn't equipped with magnetic chalkboards, you can still have a magnetic board. Purchase it at about the same cost as a flannel board, or mount any thin sheet of steel on a ¼ inch plywood.

132

Thin steel suitable for the purpose can generally be obtained from sheet metal fabricators or from furnace installers. If you want to color the surface, any flat enamel will do, but two solution epoxy enamels are preferred since the surface will be more durable.

Display Boards

Probably the oldest visual aid next to the chalkboard is the "flannelboard." The term "flannelboard" has become synonymous with "fabric board." In reality, many fabrics are used in making display boards, not merely flannel. Some of the more commonly available display or teaching board materials are flannel, felt, and flock. The newest is Velcro®. All of these fabric boards depend for their effectiveness on the intertwining of fibers of the board covering with the fibers on the cut-out or aid. Often the nap of one fiber will entwine with another, but the best way to be certain is to try it out.

Felt Board. Pieces of felt will invariably adhere to each other. So, if you wish to use a felt board, the practical thing to do is use felt cutouts also. There's a big advantage in such a selection, for felt is relatively easy to use. It has body to it, yet it's not difficult to cut into complex silhouettes. The variety of colors in which it is available is an immense instructional plus factor. Its dense nature will permit the use of semimoist adhesives if you wish to make permanent attachment of one part of a cutout to another (as, for example, rings around a cutout of Saturn, or apples on an apple tree).

The disadvantage to the felt board is its cost. A high quality felt can be fairly expensive, but, if you amortize it over a teaching career, its cost is but pennies a year.

Flannelboard. The base material of the flannelboard is a heavy nap flannel. Aids may be made of thin tagboard and backed with flannel. In making your own cutouts for the flannelboard you must be careful not to soak the flannel which you glue to the back of the aid—lest the flannel fibers stiffen and become useless for your purpose.

If you choose to make and glue your own, the best method would be to secure an adhesive which is liquid when applied, but which dries to a pressure sensitive *dry* adhesive.[3] This could be applied to the back of the *aid;* later, when the liquid has dried, the flannel could be applied without any possibility of saturation.

---

[3] Such as 3M's Spray-Ment® or Adhesive Product Corporation's Self-Stix®.

Some teachers use a coarse sandpaper for a backing material. In this method, the grains of sand hook onto the fibers of the flannelboard and cause the aid to adhere. While it might be quick and inexpensive, the adhesion provided by the sandpaper method is poor. The use of sandpaper as a backing material is recommended only when nothing else is available.

You can make your own flannelboard quite inexpensively—and make it double as a tackboard too. From your local lumber dealer, obtain a sheet of wood fiber underlayment—such as Celotex or ½" wallboard. Cut it to the desired size. Then attach the flannel to the board. This is best done by coating the board with a pressure sensitive adhesive or by using thermal mounting tissue or spray. (See mounting pictures, p. 170). Flannel should be a high nap type, and should be stretched taut when being applied.

Flockboards. Flock [4] is a short staple fiber—or a mixture of different fibers—which is applied to an adhesive coated surface. Greeting cards using flocked areas are quite common. You can identify a flocked surface by the "stiff velour" feeling it gives to the touch.

Although flocked boards are uncommon, flocked parts for use on flannelboards are widespread. Almost all commercially available aids use flock for a backing—primarily because its commercial application is simple and inexpensive.

Making your own flockboard is easy. All you need is flock, a board (plywood or hardboard), a paintbrush, and a brush-on pressure sensitive adhesive. Apply the adhesive to the board and allow to air dry to a soft-dry state. Dust the surface with flock, pat down lightly, and your board is finished.

Flock backed aids are made in exactly the same manner. You'll find this method far less expensive than buying sheets of "velour" (actually flocked) paper to glue to your cutouts.

You can make your own flock backed paper quite inexpensively, too. At the close of local political campaigns there are likely to be some left-over auto bumper stickers available. Get whatever the campaign headquarters will give you. Peel off the backing paper and apply flock to the pressure sensitive adhesive backing. Now you have your own flocked paper which can be glued to cutouts.

There is one caution which should be observed in using flocked materials. Be certain to back *enough* of the aid's reverse side with flock. Unlike magnetic aids—where a magnet at one spot can hold an entire 9"

---

[4] Generally available in larger art supply stores.

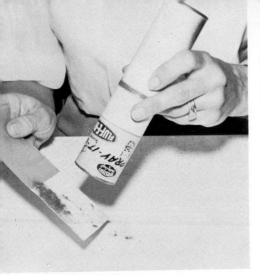

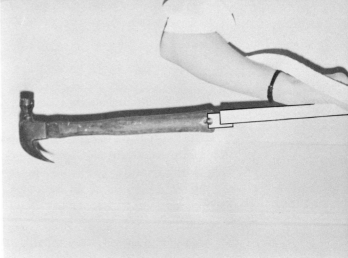

Fig. 7.5—Fibers sprinkled on pressure sensitive adhesive coated paper create an excellent "velour paper" for backing flannelboard cutouts.

Fig. 7.6—A short section of Velcro® hook material tacked to a hammer holds tenaciously to a strip of loop fabric. This same principle can be used to display heavy objects on bulletin boards.

disc—a flocked aid should be backed as completely as possible with fiber. If you observe this simple caution, your cutouts should adhere quite well.

Velcro Board. Most fabric boards operate best when the top edge is tilted back slightly to lessen the effect of gravity—or more precisely, to use gravity as a force to help keep your cutout aid *on* the board rather than one to pull it off the board.

But, if your board must be upright, or if you must display weighty objects, your answer is Velcro® board. A square inch of contact area on a Velcro board can support as much as 5 pounds of materials placed on the board. Since the Velcro system involves a positive intertwining of fibers (not accidental as with the flannelboard) you can be certain that your aid will hold on—as long as it does not exceed the weight limit of the Velcro contact area.

The Velcro board has a drawback too—cost. It is about three times more expensive than a flannelboard. Still, if your instruction involves the display of three-dimensional objects, the Velcro board is well worth the added cost.

The board section is covered with small nylon loops. The other half of the Velcro system—stiff nylon hook fabric—may be attached to your aid by adhesive, stapling, tacking, or sewing. The method you use depends largely on the weight of the object or aid you wish to attach. The type of connection must be strong enough not to break apart under the load.

Try Pegboard for Display. Certainly you've seen it done in supermarkets, so why not try using pegboard as a classroom display medium.

A variety of hooks, shelves, and specialized devices make pegboard a natural for quick display.

Perforated hardboard is generally found in two sizes, ⅛″ or ¼″ thick. The holes are usually the same size as the board thickness. One or both sides may be smooth-surfaced. If both sides are to be seen, then you should use dual smooth surface board. Always purchase a good quality hardboard, for cheaper boards flake off easily, making them useless as receptacles for pegboard hardware.

Do you have to select and mount your own perforated hardboard? What type should you choose? How should it be mounted? For most classroom use, ⅛″ double surfaced pegboard is adequate. Hardware is less expensive than the ¼″ variety, but it will nevertheless hold just about everything you need to place on it.

For wall mounted pegboard allow a ⅜″ space behind the board since most hardware requires that much space for insertion into the holes. Special hardware is available which permits mounting the hardboard directly on the wall. The offset from a wall can be achieved by the use of furring strips beneath the board, but the better method uses ⅜″ metal or fiber tubes as spacers to raise the board away from the wall.

Although some pegboard comes pre-painted, most often you'll have to paint your own. Do not use a brush, since brushing will cause the holes to fill. Either a spray can or a paint roller will perform admirably. If a spray can is used, apply several coats and spray from about half again the distance recommended on the can during the first coats. This will lessen the absorption which pegboard tends to have.

Making a Portable Pegboard. In smaller sizes, ¼″ pegboard is rigid enough to support its own weight and that of small objects. An ideal stand can be purchased in your local hardware store as standard shelf brackets. Attach the shelf brackets to one of the longer sides. If you wish to add even more sturdiness, the bottom part of the shelf bracket can be screwed to a piece of ¼″ shelving board (white pine).

Uses of Pegboard. Perforated hardboard has many applications in the classroom. Some are temporary, but the majority opinion seems to treat pegboard as a semipermanent display medium. The leading advantage of perforated hardboard over other types of display and bulletin boards is its ability to support substantial weight. Books, realia and other objects can be shown with ease. And change is just as simple; remove a hook from one place, insert it in another.

You can make geometric display shapes on pegboards too. Elasticized tape or cord of a color that contrasts with the pegboard, can be stretched over dowel pegs to form various shapes. The technique can be used for display or in actual instruction.

Pegboard also serves as an excellent base for the construction of some permanent instructional tools. The pre-drilled holes simplify project construction since a pair of pliers and a screwdriver are often the only tools required.

How To Make a Circuit Board [5]

Rare is the elementary teacher who to herself has said, "*Never* have I been tangled in wires during a electricity lesson!" Most of us have had

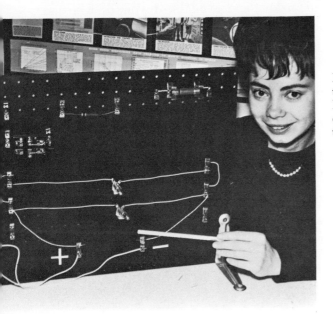

Fig. 7.7—Electrical instruction at all elementary grade levels is simplified by using a circuit board for demonstrations.

that experience. Actually, circuitry is amazingly simple—if you use a circuit board.

The circuit board has two outstanding advantages: ease of electrical connection and visibility (demonstrations can be seen by the whole class, not just the children in the front row).

Connections are easily made, in full view of your class, by using Fahnestock clips. To operate a Fahnestock clip, just press it down, insert the stripped end of a wire, and your connection is made.

[5] H. E. Scuorzo, "How to Make a Circuit Board," *Grade Teacher*, Teachers Publishing Corp., October, 1962, p. 8 ff.

Placement of parts on the circuit board is not critical. You can plan your own layout according to the demonstration circuits you will use, and arrange your clips and hooks accordingly.

The electrical components (lamp sockets, coils, electromagnets, and so forth) may be hung on the perforated board base with hooks and other devices. A trip to your local hardware store will reveal a variety of perforated board hooks adaptable for circuit board use.

Although the circuit board was designed primarily for demonstration use, it soon became apparent that pupils would gain a great deal of firsthand knowledge of DC circuits if permitted to set up their own. For the sake of battery life and fewer short circuits, draw a few wiring diagrams on index cards and make them available to pupils who use the board.

The only tools used in building the circuit board shown in the illustrations were a screwdriver, pliers, wire stripper, socket wrench and ³⁄₁₆″ drill. Construction is a one-evening project. Try it!

Parts List

⅛″ Perforated board (approx. 18″ x 24″)
14 Fahnestock Clips, with #8 mounting hole (Walsco Part #H594F)
Machine Screws, #6-32 x ¾″
Nuts and lock washers for screws
4 Shelf brackets, 6″
1 Knife switch (DPDT would be most versatile)
3 6-volt, #47, bayonet base
3 Bayonet sockets for bulbs
10′ Hookup wire, #18 or #20, solid (ordinary bell wire will do, but radio hookup wire—Belden type 8041—is easier to use since insulation strips off quickly)
1 6-volt screw terminal battery (RCA type VS 040S, or Burgess F4BP, or equivalent)
Miscellaneous circuit components (Resistors, bulbs, coils, fuses, and so forth)
Tools: wire stripper, socket wrench, pliers, screwdriver, drill (³⁄₁₆″)
(Supplies available from hardware, electronics or radio parts dealers.)

Place shelf brackets next to perforated board as shown. The front brackets should be close to the vertical edge of the board. Rear brackets will have to be inset from the edge about an inch since the holes in standard shelf brackets will not line up with each other when the brackets are placed back-to-back. Mark the location of front and rear bracket holes on the perforated board. Drill ³⁄₁₆″ holes at these points. Attach brackets with #6-32 machine screws, lock washers and nuts (see

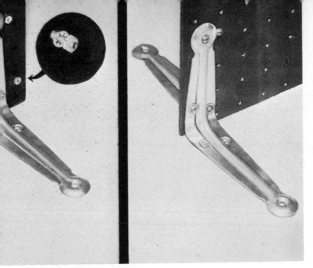

Fig. 7.8A—Making
a Circuit Board.

Fig. 7.8B

inset above). The heads of all screws should appear on the front of the board; the lock washers and nuts on the rear.

Fahnestock clips should be attached by screwing them firmly to the perforated board as shown in the diagram. They will usually be used only as junction points, and may be placed as indicated in the title photograph. Two of the clips are marked "plus" (+) and "minus" (−) for attachment of the DC power supply—in this case, a six-volt screw terminal battery.

If you wish to have any component permanently attached to the circuit board, bring each terminal in the device out to a Fahnestock clip. This will eliminate the need for any screw attachment of wires while the board is being used for demonstration. The wiring from the permanent device to its Fahnestock clip should be clearly visible so your students will be able to trace circuit continuity easily. Good electrical connection is obtained by looping the permanent connecting wire around all anchor screws just beneath the head.

Temporary attachment of electrical components (bulbs, switches, electromagnets, and so forth) may be accomplished with ordinary perforated board hooks. If the component has a suitable hole (as the bulb in the photo), just place it on the hook and hang it in place on the circuit board. If it is impractical to drill a 3/16″ hole in the component, the part may be permanently attached to the hook with epoxy glue. This circuit board shows that equal current flows in parallel circuit branches when the same bulbs are used in both branches.

This 3-branch parallel circuit hookup may be used to show that the current flow in any leg is dependent only on the impressed voltage and the resistance in that leg. Bayonet sockets and type 47 6-volt bulbs were used. By merely pulling the wire at point "X," your pupils will see that

139

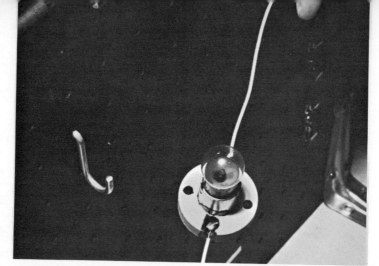

Fig. 7.8C

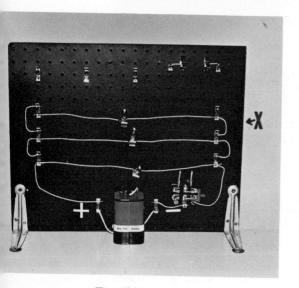

Fig. 7.8D

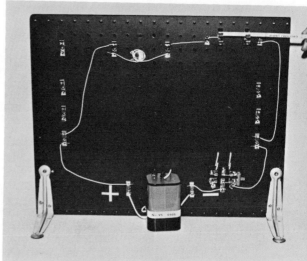

Fig. 7.8E

Fig. 7.9—Pictorial Diagram of Question Board.

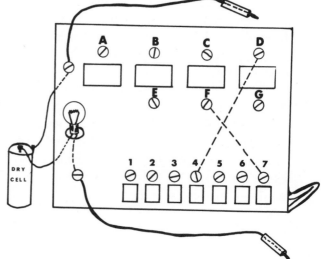

the elimination of one branch in a parallel circuit does not affect the brilliance (or the current flow) in the other legs.

The circuit board may be used for testing the conductivity of various materials. Here, a wooden pencil is placed across the open terminals in a series circuit, and the bulb does not light. If the material had been conductive, the bulb would have illuminated with an intensity dependent on the resistance of the material being tested. A brass or copper bar would provide a bright light, but a carbon rod from the positive pole of a dry cell would permit a dimmer glow. If you wish, a milliammeter, hung by perforated board hooks, could have been connected in series to show the exact current flow.

The Question Board

Want to set up a quiz board? When pegboard is used the task becomes simple, and the only tools needed are wire cutter-strippers, screwdriver, and pliers. The board can be adapted for use in as many subject areas as you wish. The correct answer indicator can be a visual or an auditory device (most teachers prefer the visual indicator for individual pupil use).

The wired question board is merely a simple series circuit. Connections are best made with Fahnestock clips and solid #18 wire, since changes in answer location can then be made without any tools at all! Such changes are desirable since pupils may learn the *location* of the correct answer.

The terminals, as indicated for wiring purposes by A, B, C, etc. are merely 6-32 x ¾" machine screws. Washers may be used under the screw head to broaden the contact area so that pupils will be able to use the device more easily. On the reverse side of the pegboard, a Fahnestock clip is placed on the screw before the lock washer and nut are added and tightened down. Of course, you can have as many sets of terminals as you wish by just adding them in the same manner.

Next to be attached to the board is the dry-battery-indicator unit. A six volt lantern battery with screw terminals will be quite long lasting, and need not be attached to the pegboard itself.

Bulletin Board

The Bulletin Board is a means of communication. Usually it is intended to give important information, to create a mood, or to lead a person to action. Often the three uses overlap. Regardless what the purpose may be, if the board does not communicate well, it is a failure.

To accomplish effective communication a bulletin board must first attract attention. Proper use of color and materials, suitable arrangement of parts, unusual content, and originality are key factors in attention getting. Once having attracted the viewer's gaze, the bulletin board must hold it long enough to deliver its message. (It is here that most "clutter" boards cease to be bulletin boards.) The last characteristic of a bulletin board is that it must have the desired reaction (inform, create mood, lead to action).

Bulletin Board Construction. If you are amply supplied with bulletin board space, you probably won't have to make your own. But thousands of teachers aren't so fortunate, and you might be one of them.

Size is a factor determined largely by your individual situation. Generally bulletin boards will range from 24″ to 36″ to as much as 4′ x 12″. A 4′ x 8′ or 3′ x 6′ board is ideal for most display work.

The board should be made from soft material such as Celotex or wood fiber wall board—soft enough so that thumb tacks and staples may be easily used and removed. If possible, the surface should have good recovery (as cork does) so that it will spring back into place without showing unsightly holes. Some teachers suggest that 9″ x 9″ *genuine cork* floor tiles be glued to the surface of the wood fiber bulletin board. Others glue colored burlap to the board to serve as a tack hole mask, and still others spatter-paint the board to camouflage any holes. Though any method will do, the first is quite expensive, and the last, while most inexpensive, serves quite well.

Always frame your bulletin board if you want a finished appearance. An unframed board gives the impression of being merely "slapped together," when in actuality you probably spent a great deal of time on its construction.

Bulletin board location is important too. Don't spend a lot of time making a board which will be hidden behind a door or in an unused corner. Rather, it should have a place of honor in classroom or hallway. It should be in the mainstream of traffic, but should have ample room for viewing. If your bulletin board is well placed, the viewer can see it easily—uninterrupted by persons passing before him.

Bulletin Board Themes. You don't have to go far to find a topic for a bulletin board display! The calendar alone is replete with them, especially major holidays, such as Lincoln's Birthday, Easter, Flag Day, and the like. But don't settle for the major ones alone. Use some other holiday themes which are significant, but little known, as Crispus Attucks Day or Pulaski Day.

Weeks and months, too, provide ample themes. Dental Health Week, Book Month, even National Hot Dog Week can provide a good bulletin board. (For the last one, an entire consumer education lesson could center around what's really in a frankfurter.)

Seasons are not to be left out in the cold. All four seasons provide excellent display board possibilities.

Your own course of study is probably the best source of bulletin board ideas. Close correlation of a bulletin board display with a subject being taught in class can serve to reinforce instruction, or, if displayed before the topic is studied, to create interest in it. If you're using it for motivation, try to leave the design open-ended as a stimulus to provoke pupil thought on the topic.

Try to change bulletin board displays at reasonable intervals. To some extent this will depend upon the theme. One teacher used Seasonal Change as a theme, and bulletin board change merely involved changing parts to correspond with the seasons. But, if, on the other hand, the theme is about Washington's Birthday, the bulletin board will probably serve little purpose if left on view till mid-March. The "change-it-every-two-weeks" theory makes little sense, too. If the subject is stale—remove it. But if there's still substantial life left in the display, leave it alone.

You might consider leaving a blank space for a while. That too can

Fig. 7.10—A good Bulletin Board display often leads the viewer to the desired action.

have great value. Pupils who never stopped to look before may halt to muse, "Doesn't something belong here?"

Or possibly you could use a monochrome background with only a single, cryptic word. It works well in advertising, and can be used to create interest in a forthcoming bulletin board theme.

Making a Bulletin Board Display. After you've selected a theme for your bulletin board, you're ready to enter the first working stage, planning.

Planning. First determine how you wish to show your theme to your audience. Think of some good billboards you've seen lately. Were they simple and clear—or complex and cluttered? The answer to that one is a great help in your first stage of planning. Lay your story or theme out on a sheet of drawing paper in approximately the same proportions as your bulletin board display.

How did you want your story to run? Left to right? Outside to center? Center to rim? Which method will best depict your topic?

If, for example, you are showing the products which are derived from petroleum, "center-out" is the logical way, since all parts are subordinate to petroleum. But suppose your bulletin board is long and narrow, then an array of products dropping from the long word "Petroleum" might be the better way. You must make the decision in each different set of circumstances.

Consider too, the colors you'll use in your bulletin board. In general, light colors should be against a dark background, or dark colors against a light one. Complementary colors are usually more effective than colors adjacent to each other on the color wheel. Traditional colors are to be preferred to the bizarre.

For example, orange against a red background leaves much to be desired. So too, orange and brown would be avoided in a Christmas display—though fully acceptable in an autumn scene.

Try to strategically place color; don't merely let it fall where it may. It is a tool, to be used wisely, not a device to increase clutter. Unless there is some overriding reason for having great variety, try to limit yourself to a background color and—at most—two or three major contrasting colors.

The keys to proper color use are within your own grasp—and you don't even need an art text. If you're able to answer "yes" to each of these criteria, you'll seldom go wrong:

1. Is there strong color contrast?

2. Are the combinations pleasing to the eye?

3. Is the overall effect striking?

Remember too, that in bulletin board work strong saturated colors are usually far more effective than weak pastels.

Organization. Part of the planning stage which is intimately connected with layout is organization. Not only must the bulletin board's layout *look* pleasing, it must make sense intellectually. A hodge-podge of material, disorganized and disjointed, does not make a bulletin board. Eliminate any idea which doesn't directly fit the theme.

Pictures and other materials should be arranged aesthetically and neatly so that they contribute to the overall theme.

Although a bulletin board is essentially a two-dimensional device, there are techniques by which a third dimension may be achieved. Die cut letters may be stuck to thumb tacks with household cement. Push the tacks only part way into the bulletin board, and your letter has a "stand-off effect." The same can be done with cutout paper letters and straight pins. Push the pin through the letter so that only the head is seen on the surface of the cutout. Then push the pin part way into the bulletin board. The same technique may be employed for other components which should have a "stand-off" quality. Often objects can be glued directly to the background paper in order to achieve a more realistic effect. Popsickle sticks make an excellent picket fence, and cotton doubles admirably as snow. You can make a tree from real branches, and a toy rocket looks like the real thing on a bulletin board "pad." These are but a few—try some for a livelier, more interesting bulletin board.

The unpardonable sin of the bulletin board is *clutter*. **Keep it** simple. Use only very important striking materials, and few of those. It would be useful if there were a rule of thumb to avoid clutter. There is not. The best advice that can be given is, "Look at your bulletin board. Is it overcrowded? You think not. Then look again." Unfortunately, the same human failing rears its head here as we find in the slide show: Pride of Authorship. "I thought of it, so it must be right." The better course is to view your bulletin board critically, and leave on it only that which is absolutely essential to the message.

You might also want some action in your display. Small battery powered motors and lights, salvaged from children's toys are excellent for making motion props on your bulletin board. However, make certain that all wires are concealed behind the background paper.

Chapter Eight

FLAT GRAPHICS, MOUNTING, AND LETTERING

To the oft used statement, "One picture is worth ten thousand words," we should always add "... if properly made, displayed, and used."

Flat graphics fall into many categories—categories which often overlap—such as maps, charts, graphs, posters, and photographs. For example, a map may often be a photograph, or a photograph can be a chart, or a chart can be a poster—and so forth.

For practical purposes, this text refers to all types of flat graphs, except photographs, as charts.

Photographs

Photographs used in the classroom are generally of three types: Teacher or student made, prints obtained from commercial sources, or prints clipped from magazines.

The first type, photographs taken by you or your students, can be especially valuable instructionally. Photographic records of field trips or classroom activities can serve you with future classes, as well being a take-off point for discussion in the class that was the subject of the photograph. Student photographic essays on school safety, fire prevention, awakening of spring, and a host of other topics provide likely class interest. Local news events, too, are excellent subjects for the classroom photograph.

Taking and Making Pictures. To begin shooting your own photographs, you'll need certain basic equipment. The most practical "classroom" camera is the 35 millimeter single lens reflex or one of the new

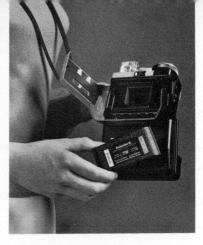

Fig. 8.1—Modern automated cameras, such as this Kodak Instamatic®, require only a click of the shutter to produce high quality photographs. Light measurement is automatic, as is lens setting. Film loading too, is no longer a chore. Feed and takeup spools are all contained in a sealed unit which is inserted bodily into the camera. (*Eastman Kodak Co.*)

"Instamatic" type cameras. A single lens reflex lets you see the *exact* picture that will appear on the film—for both you and the film view the scene through the same lens. This fact eliminates many technical parallax errors which could otherwise occur at short lens-to-subject distances. Also, your camera should be flash synchronized so that you'll be able to take pictures indoors—or outdoors when there is insufficient light. For most situations that you'd encounter, a maximum shutter speed of 1/300 of a second will suffice, as will a lens with an *f* value of 3.5. Naturally, if you can afford a higher shutter speed camera, or a faster lens, get them initially, for you'll probably find yourself "trading up" in the future if you don't.

But, if you think you're really all thumbs, buy a camera that does all but think for you. Automation has not forgotten the camera, and your local photo shop dealers will be overjoyed to demonstrate the virtues of cameras that load easily and set their own lens openings based on the film pack that's inserted and the available light. One new camera even says "yes" when you have enough light and "no" when you don't.

Remember that the average snapshot, as printed by the local drug store's photographic service, is totally inadequate for classroom use. Enlargements from your pictures may tend to be costly if you have a great many prints made. If you wish to go into black and white print enlarging yourself, it will cost a minimum of $50 for all equipment you'll need to get started. Cost thereafter is rather low. For example: An 8 x 10 inch print (the minimum suitable size for classroom use) will cost about 10¢ to make yourself. This includes developing your own film and printing the picture. Of course, it does not include amortization of your original investment. If you want to look further into doing the technical part of photography yourself, you should obtain a copy of Kodak's *Basic Developing, Printing, Enlarging,* or some similar handbook. It will give you a reasonable idea of what to expect in developing your own pictures. Contrary to popular belief, neither developing film nor printing pictures is difficult. You'll just need darkroom space, a basic enlarging kit, and patience. There's no doubt about it—the first latent image that pops forth before your eyes is enough to make you a confirmed do-it-yourself photographer.

But even if you don't want to embark on the do-it-yourself trail, you can still use photographs in instruction. Most commercial photo finishers will make an 8 x 10 enlargement from your negative for about 40 to 80¢. Mail order firms usually account for the lower prices, but you'll be sacrificing speed, since mail order service generally takes at least a week.

Photo Display. The finished photograph often takes a place of honor in any classroom display. Like any other flat graphic, photographs must be properly displayed to be effective. *Never pass photographs around the room* during your presentation or discussion. If the picture is worth showing at all, it's worth showing simultaneously to the entire group with whom you're working. But, unless the photograph you're using is large enough to be viewed by the farthest pupil, don't attempt its use. Practically speaking, this eliminates all but 11 x 14 photographs and closeup 8 x 10 prints, since a normal 8 x 10 print will seldom have images of sufficient size for classroom use. Individual pictures in a bulletin board display will generally be far more effective.

Photographs should be mounted for proper display and filing. Most magazine clippings *must* be properly mounted, lest they crumble in a relatively few years due to acidic content of paper stock.

Pictures which are too small to be seen by all your students may often be suitably enlarged for instant viewing if you use an opaque projector.

Sources of Photos. Not all photographs you'll use will be true photographs. Many will be taken from magazines and newspapers where they appear as screened "halftone" or gravure reproductions of the original photograph. Most newspaper photos are hardly suitable for inclusion in a permanent picture file, but many magazine photos are well suited. This is particularly true of large size illustrations found in magazines such as *Holiday, Life, Look,* and *Fortune.*

Photo Use Criteria. How do you determine whether a photograph should be selected for classroom use? An excellent set of criteria are suggested by deKieffer and Cochran: [1]

Suitability—will it contribute to the learning situation?

Artistic—does it meet artistic standards?

Technically correct—does it actually show what it is supposed to present?

Well composed—does it have a center of interest or is it confusing in appearance?

Clear in detail—are the details clear and meaningful or are there too many details?

Realistic—is it truthful or has it been poorly "staged?"

Size related—are there familiar objects in the picture so that students can determine relative size?

Effective in color or contrast—if color is used, are the colors true and meaningful? If black and white is used, are contrasts sharp and clear?

In making a picture *collection,* however, the first criterion must be either perpetually assumed—or completely disregarded. Seldom does a picture appear in a magazine at exactly the moment you need it in teaching! So suitability, then, must be modified to "Would it possibly contribute to any future teaching situation in which I might find myself?" Since there is no way you can be certain, it would appear sensible to collect a variety of pictures appropriate to the subject areas you normally teach.

Charts

Charts have proved to be exceptionally valuable instructional tools. The map is a form of chart, as are graphs and posters. Line drawings are often integral parts of charts, pictorials, or schematic diagrams. In fact, the range of subject matter suitable for chart-type presentation is literally limitless. Representations may be pictorial, or they may be symbolic.

---

[1] R. E. deKieffer and Lee W. Cochran, *Manual of Audio-Visual Techniques,* Second Edition (Englewood Cliffs, N.J.: Prentice-Hall, Inc. © 1962), p. 29.

Truly, a definition of the word "chart" would be difficult to propose since the word is so encompassing in modern instruction.

Chart making, then, requires a background of knowledge sufficient to let you work satisfactorily in any facet of its definition.

In chart making, you must consider certain factors:

1. *Is the subject matter satisfactory for chart-type presentation?* A great deal of complex data and large amounts of text are better presented in a text or by stencil duplication. Subjects that may be complex, but can be presented in a simplified manner, are suited for chart drawings.
2. *How should the chart be "laid out?"*
3. *What art materials and equipment will you see in chart making?*

Selection of a Base Material will be based on cost, physical characteristics, size, texture and color.

Most often, it will be some type of paperboard (cardboard). Three types of paperboards are commonly available—(1) solid, (2) pasted or laminated, (3) lined. With all other factors equal, laminated boards tend to have greater strength than solid boards. Each layer in a laminated board is referred to as a "ply." Lined boards may have a solid or a laminated core, but are surfaced on one or both sides with a paper having different qualities from those of the base.

Poster board. A paperboard lined with book paper is an excellent base material for larger charts. It can be secured with a smooth surface which will adapt well to most art mediums. The proper thickness of posterboard for display use depends on the size of your poster. If the poster is, say, 12 x 18 inches, a 60 or 75 point (1 point = 1/1000 inch) board might be adequate. But suppose your poster is 30" x 40"—then a 125 point thick posterboard would be *minimum* thickness if it is to support itself without bending.

For smaller posters—11 x 14 and below, 24 point tag stock is quite suitable. Ordinarily, tag stock is Manila colored but white can be obtained too. A good quality index Bristol can be used for small charts too.

If you're working in very large sizes, a lightweight paper or wood fiber house *construction board* may be purchased at lumber supply dealers. Standard sheets are 4' x 8', but most do-it-yourself lumber yards will cut the board down to size for you.

Another trick you can try for large charts is using *corrugated board*. Normally, this would not be recommended because corrugated board has a tendency to crease easily in the direction of the corrugation. However, you can make a corrugated board poster base which will not crease. Cut

2 sheets of corrugated board to desired size (appliance and furniture cartons are best). Coat one face of each sheet with contact bond cement and allow to air dry. Place the sheets in contact with the corrugations running perpendicular to each other. The resulting board will be quite rigid—to say nothing of being inexpensive. A white surface may be added by painting the board with white latex, poly vinyl acetate, or lucite water base flat interior wall paint. The base coat should be applied first with a small quantity of paint since a water base paint may saturate the paper and cause the corrugations to separate from the surface paper. The second coat may be normal.

Cloth has been considered an excellent chart material for hundreds of years. When it is coated with a starchlike sizing compound or a matte oil cloth (sign painters' cloth), it is an excellent surface for artwork. The distinct advantage of cloth over rigid paperboard is that it can be roller mounted for easy display. Special roll chart papers have similar flexibility and are often used as the surface material on commercially prepared maps or charts.

The *window shade chart* is an excellent device for the presentation of sequential items. The shade's roller, with its built-in rachet locks, will permit adjustment of the shade chart at any desired height.

Presentations often lose their impact unless material is presented in the right order and at the precise moment it is needed. The shade chart helps prevent premature pupil attention to information which is not under study at the moment. Then, when you need it, a tug on the shade reveals your chart instantly.

Shade charts can be changed simply. Just roll one up, lift it out of the hangers, and place the next shade chart in position for use.

Ease of storage is an important advantage, too. The end of each shade may be labeled with a title or index number and stored either flat or upright. There is never the problem of your chart tearing at folds, since folding is completely unnecessary.

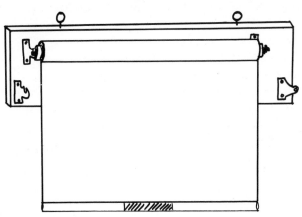

Fig. 8.2—A simple roll-up chart can be made from an inexpensive window shade. This chart is particularly valuable in displaying items which should be shown sequentially.

A hanger board, as illustrated, must be made. It is also possible to mount more than one roller at one time—thus eliminating frequent roller changes. There's an extra value built into ownership of a shade chart hanger board. You can have an emergency projection screen in your room by merely using a blank, matte white shade in the hanger board.

Rollers of different widths may be used on the same hangerboard if hangers are mounted at different levels, as shown.

In doing artwork on shade surfaces, choose your media carefully. Permanent flow pens are excellent tools, as are flexible plastic paints and rubber base interior water soluble flats. However, be careful *not* to use certain media which might flake off or crack during rolling and unrolling —such as tempera. This caution is especially true if you use plastic base shades rather than cloth, for many paints won't adhere to vinyl shade materials.

Line Drawings. An important part of any chart (diagram, map, schematic, poster, or graph) is the line drawing. A line drawing is composed of solid color areas, dots or lines. It is best exemplified by the cartoon, schematic diagram, or plan. All parts of the line drawing have the same tone unlike the continuous tone original (photograph), where color will vary continuously from black to white. A line drawing achieves more than its color-or-no-color quality by using varying line widths and spacing.

For example, shading may be achieved by using fine, closely spaced lines or dots. The illusion to the viewer will be one of shading.

On the assumption that very few teachers are able to make high quality original line artwork, techniques will be described which will help you make high quality artwork without a great deal of effort. This means that you must be prepared to use a variety of tools and art materials to help achieve this end.

Certainly the primary goal of any chart is effective communication. To this end, a clear line drawing of an operation may be superior to a photograph.

Laying Out the Drawing. A chart must be arranged in a neat, eye catching manner. A border space should be included in any line drawing. Borders on three sides should be equal, and the fourth border—the base of the drawing—should be slightly wider than the other three for a more pleasing effect. The drawing surface should then be lightly scored into quadrants to assist you in determining the most effective layout of parts. Quadrant lines, and possibly border lines, will have to be erased later, so they should be made lightly with a #3 pencil.

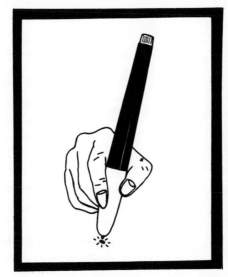

Fig. 8.3—Line drawing is crisp, but continuous tone (or half-tone) illustrations provide a lifelike effect seldom found in line art.

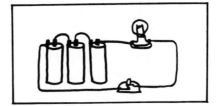

Fig. 8.4—The illustration shown at the left could easily remain without a border, for, as shown at the right, the border in no way adds to the unity of the drawing. Rather, it creates a confusion of lines. When a border holds together seemingly separate parts of a single drawing, it should be used.

Whether or not the border is erased depends on the type of drawing you are using. If the drawing consists of separate, but related parts, you may wish to use the border line to create unity among the parts. On the other hand, if the drawing already has unity by its very nature, a border would be superfluous.

Rough layout of the chart should be sketched in approximately the same proportion as the finished drawing. Try numerous possibilities before you settle on one.

Choose your wording carefully, aiming it for the intended effect. A chart may be best done in simple, factual, accurate language in showing the class donations to the United Fund. On the other hand, a poster designed to provoke action may succeed more effectively with an emotional "Uncle Sam Wants *You*," than with a staid list of benefits of armed forces enlistment.

After you have decided on pictorials and wording for your chart, you must begin actual drawing. Artwork is done in pencil—at least in rough form. You should try to use many of the mechanical aids available to you in copying art work from original or printed sources.

Transferring Artwork to the Chart. Although there are a great many methods of transferring artwork to your chart, only those which are practical for the classroom teacher are covered here. Most line copy the non-artist uses will come from advertising matter, magazines, newspapers, pamphlets and books. Some of it will be in the right size for use in your chart; most of it will not. The problem is obvious: How can you transfer artwork from source to chart—both with and without a change in size?

The enlarging square method is suitable if you have some artistic ability. For, while it is quite easy to do, the degree of similarity between your original and your copy is completely dependent on *you*. The enlarging squares method is fully described on p. 126, in relation to chalkboard use. However, exactly the same principles apply in chart making.

A pantograph can be used to both enlarge or reduce original artwork. In using a pantograph, you merely anchor the pivot point to a large drawing board and trace the original with a stylus attached to one point on the pantograph. A pencil lead in a special holder is attached to another point. The degree of enlargement or reduction is determined by adjustment of the size of the parallelogram at the center of the pantograph. Ratios are printed on the pantograph itself, so determination of enlargement or reduction is easy.

Fig. 8.5—Line drawings may be enlarged or reduced quickly with the pantograph.

The first time you use a pantograph, you may feel you've been a dismal failure. It's not so! Like any other device, the pantograph requires development of operator technique. For example, you'll soon learn that you can't cross from one side of the drawing to another, for the pencil point is crossing after you. Learn to lift both stylus and pencil point when you move from one place to another.

Also, you may need to weight the pencil point slightly in order to get a visible image. Make certain that the pantograph is *firmly* anchored, and that both your original and your chart are firmly tacked to the drawing board. The slightest position variation of any one of these three will result in distortion or double images.

So, while it is an easy device to use, you'll need some minimal skill to do an acceptable job.

Same size reproductions are very easy to transfer. Standard typewriter carbon paper can do a creditable job. You don't have to write on the original if you cover it with a sheet of tracing paper before outlining. However, some may object to typewriter carbon since it does not erase easily.

If reversal is acceptable, just make a tracing of the original with a *soft* pencil. Tracing will be easier if you use a light box. Turn the tracing paper over so that the soft pencil drawing will contact the chart. Using care not to move the tracing paper, burnish the back of it wherever a soft pencil line appears. Enough graphite will be transferred to the chart to permit "inking in" later on.

If reversal of the image is undesirable, and you don't want to use typewriter carbon paper due to difficulty of erasing, make your tracing as stated above, but, instead of inverting the paper and burnishing, invert the tracing and rub a very soft pencil over the reverse side of the tracing. Take care to cover all essential lines, at least lightly. Blackening should be as complete as possible but it is not critical. Next place the tracing, blackened side down, on the chart, and re-trace the tracing. Graphite will transfer from the blackened side to the chart. If you prefer commercial graphite, transfer paper may be purchased from major art supply stores.

Projection enlargement is the easiest way to put artwork onto your chart. Most often, the original will be small and opaque, having come from magazines and the like. Infrequently, it will be transparent. Slide or overhead projectors may be used to enlarge the transparent original, and the opaque projector is well suited to enlarging the nontransparent drawing or clipping.

Here, the small, inexpensive opaque projector ($5-$7), which is useless as an instructional tool, comes into its own. You can enlarge any line artwork from small clippings (up to 3″ x 3½″) to poster size in a jiffy. It (Magnajector) can even enlarge directly from a book without damage to pages. The projector is placed directly on the page.

Since the projection bulb is only 60-75 watts, there is practically no danger of burning the pages. Although the projected image is rather weak even in a darkened room, it is sufficient to permit tracing the image. Remember this type opaque is suited to enlarging only very small images since the entire copy opening is only 3″ x 3½″.

If you want to "blow up" larger images, an opaque projector capable of handling clippings up to 6 x 6 inches may be purchased for under $50.

For even larger originals, you can use your standard classroom opaque projector. Most will accept books, as well as clippings and objects.

In any case, opaque projection is the easiest means of transferring a drawing to your chart or poster.

If you wish to construct your own simple opaque projector, a good investment would be made in obtaining *How to Build Opaque Projectors,* a booklet which not only discusses theory of operation, but gives detailed instructions on the construction of 8 different opaque projectors. (#9314 35¢, postpaid, Edmund Scientific Co., Barrington, N.J. 08007)

Making Photos into Line Drawings. From time to time you'll come upon a continuous tone original you'd like to transfer to a chart—but as a line drawing. Commercial artists merely place the photo on a light box and a sheet of tracing paper over that. Trace any outlines or key lines and forget the details of continuous tone. After the tracing is finished, you can merely shadow in as needed with fine lines or dots. Then the line drawing can be easily enlarged to poster size.

Chart Lettering. In making any effective chart, poster or graph, good lettering is a key factor. Lettering is easy with all of the modern lettering devices available. It is impractical to try to cover all makes of lettering devices and techniques, but the means treated here are representative of the most important methods. They are:

1. Freehand.
2. Stencils and Guides.
3. Template.
4. Press letter.

Within these methods are both ink and pencil types of lettering devices. Naturally any lettering done in pencil should be inked in later.

In all types of display lettering, certain basic principles should be considered. Ease of readability is the most important. For certain special applications—such as the use of Old English on a diploma or oriental looking type in a poster designed to give a Far Eastern "feel"—it is necessary to give primary importance to letter style. But, even then, it should not be at the expense of readability. Minimum readable letter height at 30 feet is about one inch, and this is a strain on the eyes even with simple clean gothic style letters. It's always best to check the size of your letters experimentally to see if they are clearly readable at the maximum distance your chart will be viewed. Oversize letters are seldom a problem, but letters that are too small or too thin may easily ruin a chart.

Fig. 8.6—Chart letter styles which are difficult to read should seldom be used. (*Grade Teacher*)

Letter weight (thickness of line) should be approximately ⅙ to ¹⁄₁₂ of letter height and the height to width proportion of the average letter should be about 5 to 3. Optimum readability results from a clean sans serif letter, such as the sample show in Figure 8.7.

RQ A X

Fig. 8.7—Chart lettering should be clean, crisp, and easy to read, as the Gothic style shown here.

Freehand. By far, the most common type of lettering is freehand. Depending on your ability, it can be quite good or it can be extremely poor.

Unless you are extremely proficient, even freehand lettering should be laid out first in pencil in order to assure correct spacing.

Final freehand lettering can be done with any of a host of excellent devices. Most recent is the "felt" tip flow pen. Newer tips are made of Dacron, Nylon and other plastics, but the term "felt pen" has become generic for all saturated flow pens. In making single stroke letters, you are largely at the mercy of the nib's characteristics for the letter style you can achieve.

A much more accurate freehand may be obtained with the "Speed-ball"® type nib. (Fig. 8.8) These nibs are made in square, round, oval, and flat shapes to create a variety of plain and fancy letter styles. Within each nib style, there are several different size points. Style is indicated by a stamped letter: "A" for square, "B" for round, "C" for flat, and "D" for oval. Size is shown by numbers. The lower the number, the larger the letter width will be. The size a number in one style bears a close, but exact relationship to that same number in another style. Thus, nib A-O is larger than A-5, but may not appear exactly the same weight as a D-O nib.

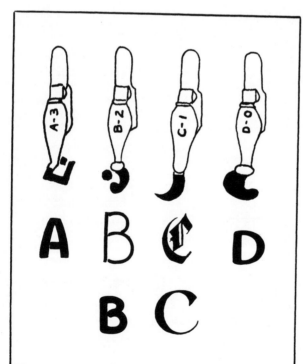

Fig. 8.8—Lettering pen nibs of different sizes and shapes make possible many types of letters.

Fig. 8.9—Straight pens with reservoir nibs are basic tools of hand lettering. (*Grade Teacher*)

Fig. 8.10—Die cut tagboard stencils are inexpensive and easy to use. (*Grade Teacher*)

The construction of the nib permits substantial lettering before it must be dipped into the ink again. A properly operating point, even in the broadest size, can hold enough ink to do at least one complete letter.

A broad spectrum of lettering ink colors is available, but black India and show card inks are favorites.

"Speedball" type nibs should always be washed thoroughly after each use, and care should be taken during washing to see that the delicate reservoir part (on which the size number is stamped) is not bent. Special feeder type nibs are available under the trade name "Speedball Flicker." In this type of pen the feeder flips back for easy cleaning.

Similar nibs are made by Esterbrook, Mitchell, Coits, and others. Special fountain-type pens may be purchased for use with Speedball nibs in order to eliminate dipping. Other pens with reservoirs are the Rapidograph, the Artbrown Freehand, and the Graphos Lettering Pens. All have interchangeable nibs.

Before you can consider yourself an expert at freehand lettering, practice is essential. Each pen type has different characteristics, so experiment first with the pen you choose. Get to know its "feel," what it can and can't do. Soon you'll find that you can't be without it in all poster work.

Stencils. Standard lettering stencils are die cut into a tough oiled or wax paper stock. Paper stencil systems usually provide some means of letter spacing and alignment since the user can't see through the stencil to judge for himself. Stenso® lettering stencils use the line-dot system. A

159

straight line is drawn in pencil on the surface to be lettered. The stencil is aligned so that the two holes just above the desired letter fall on the drawn line. A dot is placed in each hole, and the succeeding letter is spaced merely by placing its leading alignment hole over the trailing dot of the previously drawn letter.

Letters should be outlined lightly, in pencil. When the stencil is removed, letters should be "touched up" at appropriate points to avoid letting the finished product have a "stenciled look." These stencils cannot be used directly with liquid inks.

Some lettering guides (stencil type) are made of transparent plastic, and are either undercut or raised above the writing surface.

In this way, the guide can be moved laterally to form successive letters without smearing undried ink. Plastic guides of various manufacturers will produce letters from about $\frac{3}{16}''$ to $4''$ high. In the Wrico system shown in Figure 8.12 a special long nib felt pen is used. The pen itself is essential since the guide is almost $\frac{1}{4}''$ above the paper during use. Letter spacing is left to individual judgment since the guide is transparent. Alignment is achieved by placing the guide against a specially grooved straightedge, which is cork backed to prevent slippage during use. Different colors may be used, but you'll need a different felt pen for each color.

In use, a simple technique must be developed. Success will depend on your ability to keep the pen moving or off the paper. Since the ink has a tendency to saturate the paper, letting the pen rest on the paper too long in any one spot can cause seepage and result in unsightly letters.

Smaller lettering is often needed, especially on charts and graphs. A standard reservoir lettering pen and plastic lettering guides can be used by even a beginner with professional results. Drawing ink is placed in the ferrule reservoir with a dropper. A needle and plunger inside the pen are used both to keep the ink channel to the point open, and to raise the pen off the paper without smudging. Letter width up to about $\frac{3}{16}''$ can be achieved with this standard lettering pen. Plastic stencil guides must be matched to the nib size of the pen. Stencils are undercut to prevent flow of ink under the stencil.

Another lettering method frequently used by draftsmen is the *template-scriber method.* An engraved plastic template is used as a basic guide. The operator traces a stylus over the engraved letter on the template. Simultaneously a small reservoir pen in the lettering device draws the letter on your chart. This is a direct lettering method. Care must be taken, for mistakes will ruin your chart. Within limits, this

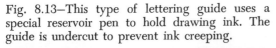

Fig. 8.11—When die cut stencils are used, the "stencilled look" may be avoided by filling in wherever appropriate.

Fig. 8.12—In the Wrico® lettering system, the stencil is raised above the writing surface to prevent smearing while using liquid inks. (*Grade Teacher*)

Fig. 8.13—This type of lettering guide uses a special reservoir pen to hold drawing ink. The guide is undercut to prevent ink creeping.

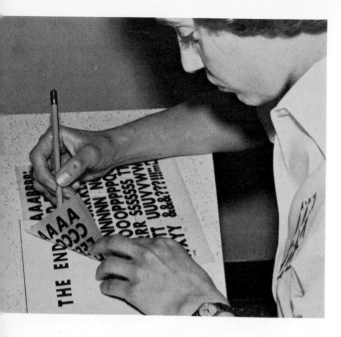

Fig. 8.14—Easy to use press-on letters are transferred from the carrier sheet to the chart by the pressure of a burnishing tool or pencil. (*Grade Teacher*)

method can produce different letter heights, slant, condensation and expansion merely by presetting a few adjustments. Excellent quality letters can be produced up to about 3″ high, depending on the template-scriber system used.

The newest and most novel lettering media is the pressure sensitive letter. Standard fonts are available in a wide variety of special faces. The letters are preprinted in reverse on a plastic sheet, and then the sheet is coated with a wax-like adhesive. Use is simple. Just place the letter bearing sheet in the proper location on your artwork and burnish the letter into place by rubbing on the plastic carrier sheet. The letter transfers easily, and no special talent whatever is needed to give professional results.

Finishing Touches on Charts. Since your preliminary drawings were probably lightly drawn in pencil, and lack contrast, you'll have to depend on other media to finish your chart, graph, or poster. The more important ones are: (1) inked line drawings, (2) inked shaded drawings, (3) colored drawings, (4) specialized pressure sensitive materials which can often achieve all of the above.

Inked Line Drawings. The inked line drawing is certainly the simplest and least expensive method of finishing your chart. It is particularly valuable in two-dimensional drawings, but can also be used with three-dimensional line art if the depth lines are not confusing.

Inking may be done with pens, brushes, or "felt" flow pens. Generally black India ink is used, but for some purposes you might want to use colored inks or flow pens.

Certain tools are needed by even the beginning chart maker for "inking in." These are (1) a standard ruling pen, (2) a triangle, (3) a French curve, (4) a template containing standard figures (circles, squares, ovals, etc.), (5) a drawing board and "T" square, (6) a ruling compass, (7) opaque white, (8) a beveled edge plastic ruler.

The ruling pen and compass have the same nib device, but vary slightly in use. A few simple rules should be followed when using either of these tools:

1. Adjust the pen wider than the line you'll need so that ink can be dropped between the blades without getting on the outer sides of the blade. Drop the ink into the pen with quill or dropper substantially *above* the point of the pen. This will keep the ink where it belongs *between* the blades and prevent large blobs of ink from flowing onto the chart. Don't overfill: ¼ to ⅜″ of ink is plenty!

2. Bring the blades together using the adjusting thumb screw. The tip of the blades should be spaced the width of the desired line.

3. Test the pen on a piece of scrap paper first. Then go immediately to your art work. Do not shake the pen, especially if fairly wide lines are being drawn, for ink could sprinkle from the pen.

4. If the pen is being used next to a straightedge, unless you're a draftsman or proficient with the tool, use a beveled edge ruler for your guide. This will prevent ink from running under the straightedge and ruining your chart. Experts are able to control the pen so that a narrow space always remains between the line and the straightedge. Under these conditions, ink never touches the ruler and consequently never creeps or smears. Until you qualify as "expert," use a beveled edge ruler, and be safe!

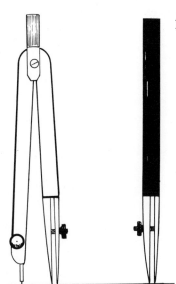

Fig. 8.15—Ruling pen and compass.

Fig. 8.16—Correct ruling angle.

5. In using the ruling pen, draw the pen along the straightedge at a 60-70° angle with the *point trailing the* handle. Never try to rule "point first."

6. Never leave the pen or compass in one spot on the paper. Keep it moving or raise it. Move the pen at a constant rate of speed, since line width may vary according to speed.

7. When using templates and curves, use undercut (beveled) varieties if they are available. If you can't find them (since professional draftsmen wouldn't need undercut guides), you can raise the template off the surface of the artwork with a 1/16″ sheet of cardboard, or, more preferably, clear plastic.

8. *Immediately* after use, clean the pen nib. A high quality, relatively lint free absorbent tissue will do, though professionals often use chamois or soft cloth. Clean all dirt from the nib.

Naturally, colored drawing inks may be used wherever India ink is indicated.

Other Methods. Lining is not restricted to the ruling pen and compass.

Flowpens may also be used for ruling and outlining drawings, but fineness of line and variable control of weight is not possible. In many cases—especially in artwork where exactness of line is not critical, felt pens and Speedball-type points are excellent tools for "inking in." This would be true, for example, in drawings of plants and animals—as opposed to graphs, plans, or patterns.

When using India ink on a pure white surface, minor mistakes can often be corrected with "Opaque White," which is sold by art supply stores under a variety of trade names. A jar of opaque white and a #00 sable brush are invaluable tools for use on the slight India ink smudge which won't erase well, and ruins the poster. Merely apply small quantities of opaque white to the error with the sable brush. In most cases, the correction will not be visible to the viewer, since, at worst, it is merely white on white—thus of such poor contrast that the error is effectively hidden.

Shaded Drawings. You can give a more professional quality to your line drawings by the addition of shading. Shading is generally of 3 types: dot, line, or continuous tone. In each of them, the same basic principle is followed. With only a little practice even a novice can do creditable shading by the first two methods, dot and line. The theory is simple. Although a line drawing of an object may have only two dimensions, the illusion of depth may be given by shading. First, imagine your two-dimen-

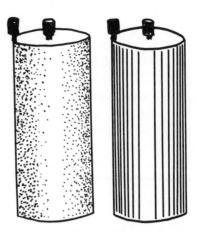

Fig. 8.17—Dot and Line Shading.

sional figure to be an actual 3-D object. Next let an imaginary light shine on it angularly from your point of view. The parts of the object which would then be in deepest shadow become black in your 2-D shaded drawing. The brightest part of the object remains white in the 2-D drawing. Between the two—white and black dots or lines may be used to create the depth illusion. Dots are made all the same size. However, they are spaced wide apart near the brightest part of the figure and closer together as you approach the deepest shadow part of the drawing. With line shading, you may use lines of constant width and variable spacing, or variable width and constant spacing, or a combination of the two.

Continuous tone shading may be produced with pencil, watercolors, or airbrush. Pencil shading is not too difficult, but it will never give the amount of intensity generally needed for chart or poster work.

To shade by pencil, first obtain a variety of drawing pencils in series, e.g., #4B, 2B, HB, 2H, 4H, 6H. Start with the hardest (6H), work with the side of the pencil point and shade the entire area which would eventually be shaded. Next, with the 4H (next softest) shade the entire remaining area from the 4B line to the darkest region. Continue on through your entire series. Pencil shading must always be sealed with a spray fixable to prevent smudging.

Watercolor shading is done in much the same manner as pencil shading but is extremely difficult to accomplish. Unless you are very skilled in the medium's use, avoid it. Airbrushing, the final method does an excellent job, but some practice is needed (See Airbrushing, p. 52).

Coloring charts and posters is done with tempera paints and brushes, or with colored inks, as stated above.

Using Pressure Sensitive Materials in Chart Construction. In recent years, pressure sensitive tapes and transfer material have eliminated much time consuming detail work.

165

The simplified method of chart construction shown here requires little (if any) drafting ability. Most graphs can be made by "drawing" with modern pressure sensitive tapes instead of pen and ink.

Specialized tapes are made in an almost endless variety of sizes, colors and patterns. There are even tapes which follow *curved* lines. And if you make a mistake, accidentally placing the tape where it doesn't belong, just pull it off. The pressure adhesives used are designed to permit easy tape removal without damaging your chart. To know how enjoyable tape drawing really is, just follow the three steps shown in the photographs.

Steps in Chart Making

1. Unroll a length of tape of the pattern or color desired. Place the end of the tape approximately one inch beyond the starting point and continue to unroll the tape out to the desired length.

2. To cut tape, place a cutting edge (or a single-edge razor blade) at the desired cut-off point. Pull the roll of tape diagonally against the cutter edge or blade. If a cutter is used, pressure of cutter against tape should be fairly heavy to avoid slippage.

3. Make a mistake? Carefully peel off tape at a 45 degree angle.

Steps in Chart Making (*Chart Pak, Inc.*)

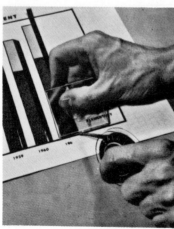

Fig. 8.18

Fig. 8.20

Fig. 8.19

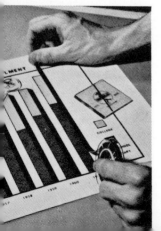

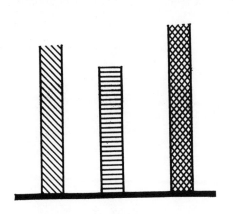

Fig. 8.21—Bar Graph. (*Grade Teacher*)

Fig. 8.22—Column Graph. (*Grade Teacher*)

The tape will leave the chart without leaving adhesive deposit or tearing the material.

The most basic chart you can construct is the *bar graph*. All that's needed is a narrow vertical tape for a reference line and a horizontal bar of tape to show each quantity. The bar may be colored or patterned, depending on your desire.

Another graph, the *column* type shown is merely a bar graph turned 90 degrees with another variable reference line added—usually a time line. Here the columns may have to be in color or pattern since they will often represent different factors. A key or legend should be included unless that which the column represents is absolutely and unquestionably clear—a possibility which is quite remote in most chart construction.

The *line graph* is actually an extension of the column graph. The columns are omitted, and the points which would be at the top center of each of the columns are connected by line segments—thus the name "line graph." By using tapes of different colors, widths or designs, plainly visible comparisons may be made on the same chart. When the data

Fig. 8.23—Line Graph. (*Grade Teacher*)

Fig. 8.24—Surface Graph. (*Grade Teacher*)

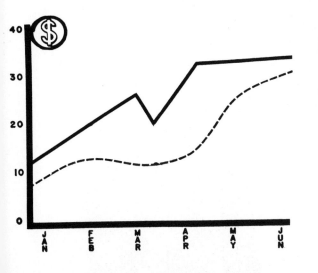

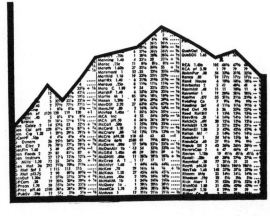

Fig. 8.25—Pie Graph. (*Grade Teacher*)

being presented must, of its very nature, be a curve (as in a normal curve, frequency distribution curve, and so forth), curve-line tape provides the answer. It can make gentle curves with as much ease as a straight line!

If you wish to show pictorial and statistical data at the same time, the *surface graph* may be for you. Actually, a surface graph is merely a single line graph with pictorial or design representation added for impact purposes. In the graph shown, a portion of the stock market report has been added to enhance interest. All this is fine, as long as you don't go too far. When the viewer is more interested in the pattern or pictorial matter than he is in the graph, you will have defeated your purpose.

The final type of chart is a familiar one in many elementary classrooms—the *circle* or *pie graph*. While it is very limited device for statistical presentations, it is most valuable as a teaching tool for the elementary school teacher. Can the tape method be used to make a circle graph? Of course it can! The curve-line tape mentioned above can be formed into a circle with a diameter as small as two inches! The addition of pictures or surface patterns, as shown, is often just what's needed to give that "professional" touch!

All in all, the tape method of chart construction has much to commend it. You'll never know how much—until you try it! [2]

Literally thousands of different symbols are commercially available in pressure sensitive tape sheets, and die cut pieces.

Tapes and plastic films, screens, and patterns are available in solid colors, both opaque and transparent. Standard tape sizes are in steps

[2] Herbert E. Scuorzo, Adapted from "Chart Construction Made Easy," *Grade Teacher*, Teachers Publishing Corp., March, 1964, pp. 38-39 ff.

from ⅟₃₂″ patterns on ¼″ tapes to 2″ tapes. Sheet sizes range from 8″ x 10″ to about 11″ x 15″. Both tapes and films may be purchased in glossy or matte surface finishes. Matte tapes and films cut down on surface reflection.

Similar patterns and symbols are available in pressure sensitive transfer sheets and are applied by the burnishing method. Some transfer symbols are available on rolls also.

To shade, pattern, or color large areas, place the thin patterned film or color tint on the chart over the area to be covered. Cut away the plastic sheeting from parts not to be covered, and remove this excess.

Special adhesive permits easy removal as long as pressure is not exerted on the parts of the sheet to be removed. The remaining film is then burnished down and becomes practically invisible. Only the color or pattern appears to be present when film is used within an outlined area.

Shading film may be positive or reverse. Normally, positive film is printed in black and applied to shade white surfaces. Reverse shading film is printed in white, and thus shades any black area.

Posters almost always include

Fig. 8.26—Typical pressure sensitive symbols that may be used on charts and graphs to lessen intricate line drawing.

Fig. 8.27A—Reverse shading film may be used to subdue backgrounds, thus giving a more vivid, almost three-dimensional look, to the main subject. (*3 M Company*)

Fig. 8.27B—Reverse and positive shading applied to the same word, side by side, show the effects which can be achieved with each type of film. (*Chart Pak, Inc.*)

pictorial representation. Instructional graphs should, too, but seldom do. Appropriate magazine, catalog and newspaper cutouts are often excellent additions to charts. Not only can they add significant color, but they can raise the interest level of an otherwise dreary chart. Cutouts should always be mounted neatly.

Mounting Pictures and Objects [3]

Teachers are keenly aware of the need for using pictures and objects as instructional aids. For effective use, many of these materials must be properly mounted for display. You will have to consider such factors as color harmony, picture placement, and lettering in order to produce an effective product.

The most frequent type of mounting encountered in the classroom is that of flat pictures—usually photographs or illustrations clipped from magazines. In order to increase the useful life of such pictures they should be mounted on a sturdy backing material (such as heavy tag stock or chipboard).

Dry Mounting. Flat pictures and cloth articles are often mounted by the "dry" method. Dry mounting is usually done in a special heated laminating press, but it may also be accomplished using an ordinary household clothes iron.

When mounting tissue is used, the tissue is placed between the picture and the mount board, and laminated under the heat and pressure of the press.

To dry mount without a press, a mounting spray or tissue may be used as the adhesive. An electric iron becomes a practical substitute for the mounting press, as shown in the illustration.

Dry mounting may also be used with thin, flat materials other than pictures or cloth—such as leaves. Naturally, any material or picture which would be decomposed by the 220-degree heat of the electric iron should not be mounted by the dry method. Care should be taken to apply exactly the right amount of heat for the correct length of time (usually about 10 seconds). Too little heat will result in poor adhesion, and too much will cause buckling.

There are dry mount adhesives in the form of a liquid which may be brushed on, but they are currently available only in bulk quantities.

Wet Mounting. In true wet mounting, the entire reverse side of the picture and/or mounting board is coated with a liquid adhesive,

---

[3] Herbert E. Scuorzo, Adapted from "Mounting Pictures and Objects," *Grade Teacher,* Teachers Publishing Corp., May 1962, pp. 62-63 ff.

Fig. 8.28–When using dry mounting spray, the back of the picture or clipping should be evenly coated with the adhesive and allowed to air dry.

Fig. 8.29–The clipping is then placed, adhesive side down, on the mounting board. A clean sheet of paper is placed over the clipping and pressed with an electric iron, set approximately at "rayon-wool." Press from the center to the edges, slowly, to avoid air bubbles.

Fig. 8.30–Completed dry mount picture.

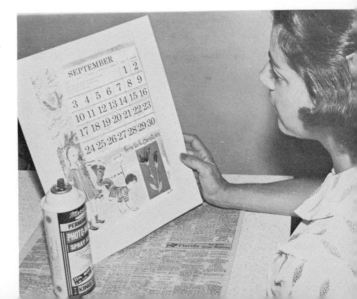

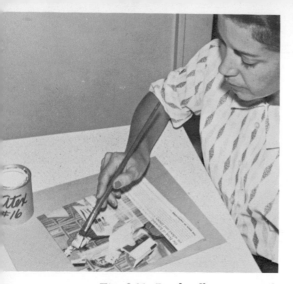

Fig. 8.31—Brush adhesive onto the back of the picture to be mounted.

Fig. 8.32—Moderate brayer pressure puts the picture into firm contact with the mount. However, adhesive may ooze from the edges of the picture being mounted. For this reason it is best to be very careful that the brayer does not exceed the edges of the picture.

usually by brushing. Ordinary wallpaper paste may be used, but it has been found that adhesives specifically designed for wet mounting give better results.

The key to wet mounting by the amateur is in the thickness of the picture being mounted. If the illustration or photograph is on fairly heavy stock, wet mounting is simple. The thinner the stock becomes, the more difficulty you will encounter. Most thin papers have a tendency to curl when the adhesive is applied, thus making them hard to handle.

If you wish to wet mount magazine illustrations, or any other picture printed on fairly thin, absorbent paper, it is a good idea to coat the reverse side of the picture with a clear acrylic spray before applying the liquid adhesive. This plastic coating slows absorption of the glue and prevents the picture from curling before you get a chance to apply it to the mounting board.

A word of caution to the prospective wet-mounter: Don't use the finest picture in your materials file for the initial attempt. A few experimental wet mounts should be tried first.

Pressure Sensitive Adhesives. For many years, the only easily available pressure sensitive adhesive materials (PSA) were cellulose tape and masking tape. Their simplicity of use has led adhesive engineers to the development of new and better PSA products which can be sprayed or brushed on, and which provide permanent mounting.

Often you may not require the degree of permanence provided by the wet, dry or PSA methods already described. If all you need is temporary display mounting of pictures, try using pressure sensitive discs, dots, tapes or plastics.

172

Pressure sensitive discs are generally coated on both faces with a waxy adhesive. The discs are inserted between the picture and the mounting surface, and firm pressure is applied to the face of the picture wherever a disc was placed. The number of discs to be used will depend largely on the size and weight of the illustration being mounted. Disc-mounted materials may often be separated without damage to either picture or mounting material. However, a waxy residue is sometimes left on the surface which came in contact with the disc. Depending on the mounting materials used, the residue may be removed with mild detergents or solvents such as carbon tetrachloride.

PSA tapes are also available with adhesive coatings on both sides of the tape. Here, as with wet mounting, experimentation is the better part of valor. Some brands of double-coated tapes are "on to stay," while others provide simplicity of removal similar to pressure sensitive discs.

The newest pressure sensitive adhesive uses tape or paper tabs only as a carrier for the adhesive. The adhesive is manufactured with a release paper backing so that when one side of the tape or dot is placed on the picture to be mounted, it adheres to the picture. Then the release paper is pulled off, leaving only pure adhesive. This system eliminates buckling which sometimes occurs with double surfaced tapes that retain the plastic carrier *between* adhesive coats.

Also in use are reusable adhesives—puttylike plastic materials which will adhere to any clean surface. These materials are of value in that they

Fig. 8.33A—Wax paper bearing the adhesive ribbon is placed on the picture or object being mounted.

Fig. 8.33B—When bearer strip is raised and removed, pure adhesive is left on the picture. It is pressure sensitive and will adhere permanently to any clean, dry surface.

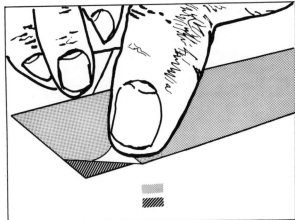

do less damage to walls than any other types of adhesive. The only evidence that this type of adhesive was used might be a mild oil-like spot at the point of application.

Mounting Objects. In learning to mount objects, the first step should be familiarization with some of the more important common adhesives. It will soon be seen that no one adhesive can serve all purposes equally well. Any of the adhesives which will be described for mounting objects could also be used for mounting pictures.

Contact adhesives are similar to rubber cement in consistency and application. Here, however, the similarity ends. While rubber cement may ordinarily be used only for paper-to-paper adhesion, contact cements may be used on almost any surfaces with broad contact area. In using these adhesives, both surfaces must be coated and allowed to air dry for a few minutes. Then the two surfaces are placed together, and adhesion is instantaneous. For this reason, materials cemented by the contact method have the advantage of being instantly available for use.

There is also the obvious disadvantage that materials once placed, cannot be repositioned. To overcome this drawback, a sheet of clean paper may be inserted between the two dry adhesive coated surfaces before they are placed to contact. After the desired positioning has been achieved, the paper may be withdrawn and the object will then be in contact with the mounting surface.

Contact cement is designed for materials with relatively large areas of mounting surface. For example, a coin display (metal to cardboard) could easily be mounted because a coin has a relatively large

Fig. 8.34—Putty type epoxy or heavy paste silicone adhesives are ideal for mounting objects since part of the object actually embeds in the adhesive, thus assuring sufficient contact area for permanent holding.

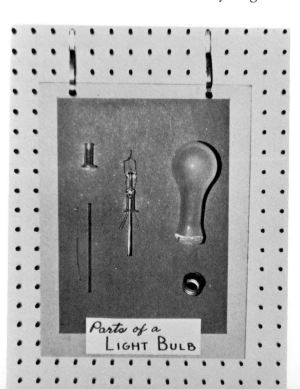

mounting surface compared to its weight. An electric light bulb, on the other hand, should not be mounted with contact cement since there is only a very small contact area compared to the weight and mass of the object.

The newest and most spectacular member of the adhesive family, *epoxy resin cement,* is being used in a wide variety of applications, from repairing damaged automobile bodies to sealing joints in swimming pools.

Epoxy resin adhesives usually consist of two parts—a resin and a hardener. Either one of the components has no adhesive quality. However, when mixed together, the molecules of the adhesive actually reach out and intertwine with the molecular structure of the materials being joined. This amazing property has prompted manufacturers to claim that one drop of this adhesive can support 2,000 pounds. While classroom teachers will have little occasion to put this to the test, the author has had the experience of trying to break a metal-to-metal epoxy bond with a hammer unsuccessfully.

Almost any materials may be joined with epoxy cement. In mounting materials or objects, however, one caution should be observed. The mounting surface selected must be strong enough to support the object being mounted. While the epoxy bond will not break, it is entirely possible for a poor base material to pull apart if the object being mounted is too heavy. In mounting objects on vertical surfaces, care should be taken to hold them in place during the curing time of the adhesive. With epoxy cements, this time is approximately two hours at room temperature. Curing is more rapid at higher temperatures, and may be reduced to as little as five minutes if mild heat is applied.

White glue is a common name usually applied to a group of adhesives having a plastic (polyvinyl acetate) base. They derive their name from the fact that they are ordinarily milky white in color. Sold under a wide variety of trade names, these white glues may all be used to join porous surfaces (paper, wood, earthenware), and all dry practically clear. Smaller sizes (up to about a pint) are usually packaged in plastic squeeze bottles and are quite handy for proper glue application. White glue may also be used for wet mounting, as earlier described.

Another familiar adhesive is *household cement.* This has an advantage of relatively rapid drying. So, if you want to mount thumbtacks to the back of cardboard die-cut letters for bulletin board use, household cement is for you. It may be easily identified by the fact that it always is packaged in a tube and has the familiar smell of nail polish remover.

Special adhesives are available for mounting various other kinds of plastics, as styrene, vinyl, mylar, and others.

Protecting Flat Graphics

When a chart is designed for one time use, there is little reason to protect it. But, when you intend to use a picture over and over again—possibly even with pupil handling—some protection is needed. The first means you might try is mounting, for damage due to handling would be considerably lessened if a sturdy *mount* were handled, rather than the picture. This type of protection is particularly valuable in the case of photographs or magazine clippings. Of course, this affords no protection for the *surface* of the graphic.

Clear Plastics offer the best possibilities. In using them to cover graphics, four general methods are used: (1) sprays, (2) heat and pressure lamination, (3) pressure sensitive adhesive "laminates," and (4) envelopes.

Sprays are suited only for the most meager type of protection. "Fixatif" aerosols provide a protective setting action to lock in chalk, watercolor, or pencil drawings. A substantial coat (really 2 or 3 light coats) can be somewhat water resistant.

Not all printed surfaces can accept acrylic plastic sprays, so test first to see that the acrylic solvent in the spray doesn't dissolve the inks in a magazine illustration. In addition, penetration of solvent can sometimes be objectionable. As a result of this penetration you may get some "see through"—that is, the illustration on the reverse side may appear through the printing stock, making your illustration useless for display purposes. To prevent—or at least lessen—"see through" on magazine stock, try spraying from at least twice the distance recommended on the aerosol can. The acrylic spray will then bear less solvent (due to evaporation during travel), and will penetrate the clipping less.

Fig. 8.35—Clear acrylic sprays provide a thin coating for light protection against fingerprints, smudges, and the like. A somewhat more durable coating is obtained with clear lacquer spray.

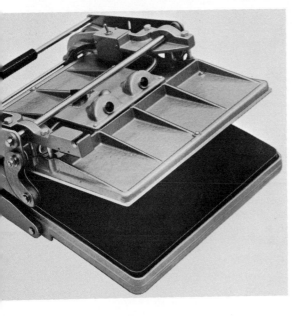

Fig. 8.36—Whether you're laminating a protective sheet of plastic to a picture, or a picture to a mount, the laminating press is the ideal tool for the task. (*Seal, Inc.*)

Laminates. The best picture protection is afforded by plastic laminating film. Lamination is performed under heat and pressure in a special press. The plastic softens during heating and is effectively bonded to the graphic being covered.

Laminating presses should be standard equipment in schools, but, unfortunately, few schools own them.

Laminating film is generally made of Mylar® polyester or acetate. Mylar film is far more durable than acetate, and does not become brittle or yellow with age. Large school-type laminating presses are able to handle materials up to 26" x 32".

To laminate in a press, the platens are brought up to operating temperature, and the graphic and plastic, sandwiched together, are placed in the press and heated under pressure for 15 to 30 seconds.

Smaller size heat pressure lamination can be achieved on thermal copy machines. The machine you use determines the size of the graphic which can be laminated. Generally, it is limited to letter or legal size laminations on flexible paper.

Pressure Sensitive Adhesive (PSA) *Lamination* requires neither heat nor special equipment. As such, it is the ideal for the classroom teacher to use on graphics to be permanently protected. It is available both in matte ("invisible") and glossy finish. Different thicknesses are available beginning as thin as .002 inch. You can purchase small cut sizes (e.g. 10" x 13"), or rolls as wide as 54 inches.

Generally, the PSA plastic needs to cover only the chart surface. However, with these adhesive coated plastics, you can completely waterproof your graphic by covering both surfaces, front and back, and allow-

177

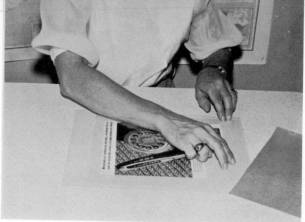

Fig. 8.37A—Release paper is peeled from the pressure sensitive adhesive coated clear plastic and readied for application to the face of the picture to receive the coating.

Fig. 8.37B—After plastic is applied, the entire surface should be burnished until it is entirely clear, and it is obvious that contact is complete. Once applied to a paper surface, the plastic cannot be removed.

ing an edge overlap where the adhesive surfaces can meet—thus completely encasing the graphic.

PSA coated acetate, mylar, and vinyl sheets are clear. Polyethelene adhesive sheets are slightly milky, but the cast does not seriously affect graphic clarity. However, the dimensional stability of polyethelene is poor, and it may shrink from the edges with changes in temperature.

Since these plastics are coated with adhesive, they are necessarily mounted on release backings.

Some of the plastics used develop high static charges and become difficult to handle. Here is the easiest method to use in mounting most flat graphics:

1. Cut a piece of plastic and release paper slightly larger than the size of the graphic to be covered.
2. Place the unit, release side up, on a flat surface, such as a table.
3. Remove the release paper, exposing the adhesive.
4. Place the graphic, "right" side down into contact with the adhesive. Do this extremely carefully, for the static charge on the plastic may draw graphic and plastic together. This difficulty generally occurs with thin graphics.
5. Burnish the plastic to the graphic with a brayer, or merely with hand pressure.
6. If only the front of the graphic is to be covered, trim the excess plastic over the edges. If it is to be covered front and back, apply another sheet of plastic, then trim, leaving a plastic margin of ⅛ to ½ inch, depending on the thickness of the graphic being encased.

Plastic envelopes, usually made of cellulose acetate provide excellent short-term protection. Their greatest benefit is that they can be

178

used over and over since they do not become a permanent part of the graphic—but merely enclose it.

These envelopes are normally used as two-sided acetate pages in presentation albums. Stock sizes are 8½″ x 11″, 11″ x 14″, 14″ x 17″, and 18″ x 24″. Sheet acetate is available in various thicknesses if you wish to fold your own protective sleeve in other sizes (.0075″ acetate is suitable for folding).

Thinner roll films, vinyl, mylar, and acetate (cellophane) may be used if the mount of the graphic is sufficiently rigid to allow the plastic to be folded around the edges of the mount and taped to the rear side.

Cataloging Pictures

Every teacher should have an instructional picture file. The methods of graphic design, photography, lettering, and mounting are all essential factors to good visual presentation, but swift recovery is important too. A simple cataloging system can be all important in proper retrieval.

Since no vast quantity of pictures will ever be required, there is no need to use the same considerations one would if the file were one for an entire school system—or even one school building.

But you must consider:

1. Subject areas to be included.
2. Storage space that is available.
3. Maximum picture size to be included.
4. Standardization of mount size.
5. Indexing.

Subjects included in your picture file should be those you teach or might teach. Those generally included are broad areas such as, Arithmetic, Health, Handwriting, Reading, English, Social Studies (Geography and History) and Science. Teachers of special subjects would probably limit their collection to their own areas, but stress collecting pictures suitable at various grade levels. In many subjects it would be necessary to have sub-divisions. For example, a middle grade teacher would probably have to sub-divide the social studies file into United States History to 1860, United States History 1860 to present, State Geography, Canada, Mexico, Central America, South America, and so forth.

Storage space and mount size are intimately related factors. A suggested size would be 11″ x 14″ since mounting stock is readily available in this size. In addition, pictures mounted on 11″ x 14″ will fit—though not upright—into a standard legal size file cabinet.

The size has further advantages in that clippings from even the largest magazines will generally fit on the mount. In case the clipping is too large, two 11″ x 14″ mounts, hinged, can usually accommodate it. Maximum flat picture size is, of course, determined by the mount size you have set as your standard. Under no circumstances should the mount be less than 9″ x 12″.

Indexing can be accomplished on index cards or in a booklet. Each system has something to commend it as well as some drawbacks.

The index card method provides flexibility, but it is no easier to locate an item by flipping index cards than it is by flipping picture mounts.

The more desirable system—though one with less flexibility in listing—lists the title of each picture by subject on one sheet numerically within each subject. As long as there is sufficient subject matter division in your original breakdown, a small classroom picture collection will probably not exceed 30 to 50 pictures—or about 2 typewritten lists— per subject, *maximum*. Keep all file index sheets together in one loose-leaf binder with subject tabs.

To find a picture, you merely (1) scan the looseleaf index tabs for the desired subject, (2) scan the subject page for the suitable title, (3) note the subject index number, and (4) locate the matching number in the file.

Folding posters that fit within the dimension maximums of the system may be filed also for easy location.

Chapter Nine

REALIA
AND MODELS

Why are realia and models grouped together? They all show actuality—either with the real object or with a representation of it.

Realia

What Is It? When an actual object is used as an instructional tool,
we call it *realia*. (By dictionary definition, the word exists only in the
plural, but in AV use it is both singular and plural.) A representation of
the object, in one of many forms, is a model. It may be larger, smaller, or
life-sized.

But what is a model for one society could be realia to another. For
example, a carved wooden African doll would be realia in the American
classroom, but it would be a model of life to the African child.

Terms do overlap, but this is of little importance. What is important is that instruction can be vitalized by using objects—real or
model!

And realia must be suitable. Merely introducing interesting objects
which are unrelated to the curriculum might be acceptable for a "Show
and Tell" session, but it is hardly suited to use in the upper grades. The
realia used should bear a direct relationship to topics being studied.

Realia are most often three dimensional, and, as such, may require
special methods of display and storage. In addition, they may be delicate,
valuable, or even irreplaceable. They may be too large, too small, too
heavy, or even unsafe for pupil use. Realia, then, pose problems which
generally do not exist with other instructional media, both in storage
and use.

Since live objects are also realia, one very special problem is apparent—the care of living things, both plant and animal.

Where to Get Realia. Teachers tend to be inveterate travelers; for this reason they are often collectors too. Armed with artifacts of world wide civilizations, they can treat their pupils to first hand experiences and objects. But there are other ways of securing realia, too.

Exchange. If you're looking for a particular item from some part of the world, there's always the possibility that a teacher over there would like to receive an instructionally useful item from your area.

How do you find the name of a teacher willing to exchange? Try *Who's Who in American Education.* This standard reference work lists biographies of thousands of administrators and teachers—with addresses. Choose one from a likely area and write. You may find a very cooperative fellow teacher.

Sponsors. Many commercial firms and associations are willing to send samples of raw and manufactured materials. You'll find such things as cotton bolls, petroleum products, wood samples, and many more are yours for the asking. Two excellent source books for free materials are *Selected Free Materials for Classroom Teachers,* by Ruth H. Aubrey (Fearon Publishers, Palo Alto, California, $1.75), and *Elementary Teachers Guide to Free Curriculum Materials* (Educators Progress Service, Randolph, Wisconsin, $7.50).

When writing to commercial sponsoring firms for materials, be reasonable in your request, and state how you intend to use the materials requested.

It is not at all unreasonable to expect that the sponsor's name or trademark will appear with the object sent to you. And, as long as it is only incidental to the educational value of the material, there should be no objection to its use in the classroom. Materials which are obviously crass commercialism should not be used.

Government. State and local governmental agencies often will provide information on where you can secure objects needed for instructional use. Very few will provide the realia itself.

Field Trips. Probably your best source of local realia is the field trip. One group may hunt for rocks and stones, another for shells, still others for leaves, fossils, etc. The realia secured locally are often the springboard to more intensive study of your own area. For example, in one class a boy brought in a small piece of sandstone with a shell imprint in it. That little discovery—in his own back yard—triggered class interest. How did it come to be? This led to a study of the area's geological past in an atmosphere of high pupil interest. Up until this time, fossil was just a word, and geological history was merely a dull phrase. With a fossil discovery by a classmate, the whole field came alive, and real learning took place.

But the "field trip" need not be local. One teacher had a friend who went mountain climbing in Mexico. As a souvenir, he brought back a piece of sulfur coated lava chopped from the cone of the Paracutin volcano. Imagine the thrill that rippled through the 6th grade class when, after discussing the birth of Paracutin and seeing a film of it, the teacher produced a piece of it for everyone to feel! Not one pupil had correctly imagined what lava looked like! Again, realia was the key to real learning.

Collections As Instructional Tools. Children have immense curiosity, and a great deal of it is often directed to "collecting." Dolls, shells, leaves, stamps, coins, and many more realia are suitable as instructional tools.

While the very act of collecting may be rewarding to the pupil, it will be far more beneficial if he can develop and learn order, critical examination, identification, classification ability, and appreciation of value.

Black Light Box. An important facet of realia collection is, of course, identification. In order to do this, many objects—particularly stamps and certain rocks—should be examined under ultra violet light so that fluorescent properties may be observed. Most fluorescent devices are quite expensive, but here's one you can build for only a few dollars and still introduce your pupils to "black light" examination of objects.

You'll need these materials:

- A corrugated board carton, about 10″ x 10″ x 14″
- A lamp switch socket with a 6″ reflector unit attached (*Not* a reflector bulb)
- Plastic white glue
- Utility knife
- 3″ gummed kraft paper tape
- Spray paint to cover carton (Unless special carton paint is used, printing may "bleed" through the spray)
- An ultra violet bulb, either GE Type AR1, or GE Type Purple-X

Follow these instructions, and you'll be using black light viewer within an hour: [1]

---

[1] Adapted from Herbert E. Scuorzo, "Let's Make a Black Light Box," *Grade Teacher,* Teachers Publishing Corp., LXXX, Number 3, p. 13 ff.

Fig. 9.1

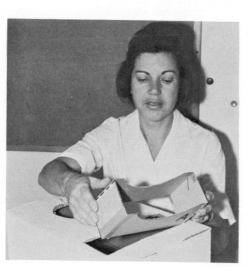
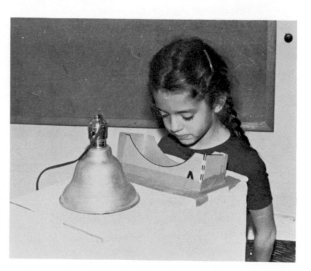

Exhibits. When suitable realia collections are made, they can be displayed in the form of exhibits. It is important that the display be well organized around a central theme, and be free of clutter. Just as "collection" of realia and all it implies, is a valuable experience for a child, so too, pupil preparation of an exhibit provides the opportunity for communicating the *meaning* of one's realia collection to others.

The value of exhibits can't be overestimated. For example, in one suburban school a pupil developed an exhibit on fuels—a simple enough project—including lignite, wood, hard and soft coal and oil. It was then the teacher discovered that some of her fifth grade pupils had *never seen* a piece of coal. Their knowledge of it was completely from books.

All items in an exhibit should be clearly labeled. Block lettering (or manuscript) is best.

184

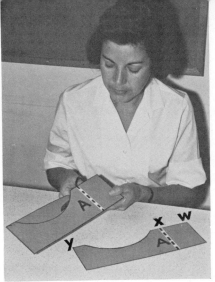

Keep in mind the fact that communication is the goal. The exhibit should be arranged for the viewer; therefore, the exhibitor must know his audience and arrange the display accordingly. It may be necessary to draw your viewer to the exhibit with posters, colorful designs, moving objects, or artfully lighted displays.

Making a Portable Exhibit Stand. You may have an exhibit mounted on flat chipboard or cardboard—intended for wall hanging—but then you find that the only available display space is on a table. You can solve the problem by making this stand:

1. Cut 2 sheets of heavy, rigid cardboard as shown in Fig. 9.2.
2. Bind the sheets with pressure sensitive adhesive cloth tape (Mystic®) along the upright edge. Put tape on both sides for best results. Leave a space between the two edges to allow the stand to fold closed.

In use, the stand is merely opened so that the two parts form about

Fig. 9.2A—All that's needed for construction of this stand is tape and two sheets of cardboard.

Fig. 9.2B—In use, the portable stand easily holds an 11 by 14 inch illustration or exhibit.

a 90 degree angle to each other, and the rigid exhibit base is placed across the two points marked "X."

Naturally, the larger you make your stand, the heavier the construction material must be. Even ¼" plywood is suitable when adequately hinged at the joining edges.

Embedding Realia in Plastic. Since some types of realia may be too delicate or too small for pupils to handle successfully in their natural state, you may want to try embedding realia in clear plastic.

Liquid casting resins are available from hobby and art supply shops, both in clear and colored forms. Or, you may use clear plastic and use special dyes for coloring the resin.

Casting resin is usually a viscous, colorless liquid which gels (solidifies) without the evolution of water or other volatile solvents. A "hardener" is added to the resin to cause the resin change from a liquid to a solid. This hardening process ordinarily takes place rapidly at 120° to 180° F, but the addition of a "promoter" chemical can cause the change from liquid to solid to occur at room temperatures.

Choice of hardener depends on the type of resin used, and the promoter, if used. Since each resin manufacturer's choice will vary, it is impossible to give specific instruction on hardeners or promoters to use. However, you'll find that resins and their associated chemicals are sold as units—the proper chemicals in measured amounts. Since proportions are critical for proper hardening, follow the mixing instructions for the resin you purchase.

Various kinds of objects can be successfully embedded in plastic. Coins, stamps, leaves, shells and other small specimens, to mention a few. The best embedment is one that does not contain moisture.

Fig. 9.3—Resin for casting should be mixed in a paper cup and poured slowly into the mold to avoid making excessive air bubbles.

Fig. 9.4—Delicate materials, such as this grass seed and fern, can be examined by pupils with no fear of damage when the items are embedded in clear plastic.

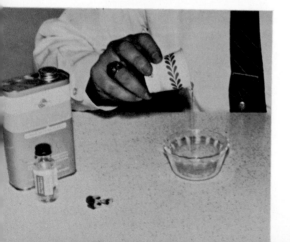

However, if you wish to embed such an object, it must first be dried. The best, and easiest way to do this is with silica-gel, a thirsty chemical which absorbs water from the object without itself deliquescing.

Resin mixing is done with popsicle sticks in unwaxed paper cups since it is extremely difficult to remove the liquid resin from utensils.

After the resin is mixed, pour a thin layer of it into a smooth glass or ceramic mold—such as an ashtray, custard cup, or refrigerator dish.

Then the resin is allowed to gel (according to manufacturer's instructions) and the object to be embedded is placed on the gelled surface. If the object is one which will float on the resin, it should be placed on the resin while the surface is still tacky in order to hold it in place. Next pour another layer of resin sufficient to embed the object.

Although most resins require elevated temperatures for curing (about 180°) the manufacturer's instructions must be followed. If 180° control is needed, it can be achieved rather easily by placing the mold in a pan of warm water and using a cooking thermometer to maintain proper temperature. Do not let the water touch the resin.

The gelled resin shrinks very slightly upon cooling, and thus removal from the mold is not too difficult. However, to separate the plastic from the mold, score the plastic with a sharp instrument at the point where it touches the mold.

Ordinarily, only the scored edge will need smoothing and this can easily be done with a very fine file. If the surface that was in contact with the air is not smooth enough for you, a little gently applied polishing compound will do the trick. The surface that was in contact with the mold will be as smooth as the mold itself, and usually does not need polishing.

Live realia. The real key to realia is using objects in such a manner that they truly impart an understanding which could not exist any other way. Plants and animals are realia when we use them instructionally.

Pet Fair. One third grade teacher planned a Pet Fair with her class. Library materials were secured by both teacher and pupils. Many students gave reports on the care of their own pets. Others drew posters depicting some desirable characteristic of pet care. The teacher used a filmstrip designed to help a student understand the responsibility that a master has for his pet. All of these activities were highly successful. Still, the use of realia was the crowning feature of the fair. With actual pets at hand, pupils were able to experience sight, sound, touch, and a variety of emotions. Certainly true learning is the sum total of all these experiences—and all exist only when realia are used.

Fig. 9.5—Working with live realia, as students do in a classroom pet fair, provides experiences unavailable by any other means. Although the exhibit itself is important, care of animals is stressed in this undertaking.

But learning with live animal realia does not stop with a knowledge of the animal itself. It opens up a whole avenue of study regarding the animal's environment, feeding, and care, whether the animal's environment be land, water or air.

Models

The need for models in formal instruction is obvious. It is not always possible to bring realia into the classroom for study. So we turn to the best representation of it—the model.

A model may be scaled up, down, or equal to "life size." It may represent part of an object, or may be an actual replica. Some models use motion to achieve their effect, others color, and still others depend on the elimination of all parts of a mechanism except the few related ones under study. This last type is generally called a mock-up.

Models are used instructionally in those situations where concrete visualization of three-dimensional objects is educationally desirable.

Fig. 9.6—Model making is no longer the chore it once was, and finished replica are far more accurate. Model kits which are suitable for class use are widely available in hobby stores.

188

In addition to the wealth of commercially available models designed specifically for education, literally hundreds of plastic model kits are available in any large toy store. Many of these are quite suitable for instructional use and your pupils will enjoy putting them together.

Styrene plastic model making from kits is vastly easier than model construction was formerly. Parts are premolded into proper size and shape. All the model maker need do is put them in the right place, and glue them together with a special styrene model cement.

Making Your Own Models. The time always comes when the commercial aid is unavailable. Then you may have to work out one of your own. The real key to instructional models is simplicity.

For example, the enlarged ruler is one of the simplest, but most valuable models you can make. In teaching linear measure, it's most difficult to see if all pupils can pinpoint $1\frac{3}{16}$ inch on their student desk rulers. But, with the enlarged ruler used as a scale model, instruction in linear measurement takes on a new dimension—pupil interest.

The Enlarged Ruler. To make your own enlarged ruler, you'll need a piece of light colored chart paper 1 foot wide and 16 feet long, and a broad tip felt marking pen. If you can't get the chart paper, just use old (but strong) window shade material, cut it to proper width and glue pieces together until you have the 16 foot length. Then draw your ruler to scale on the chart roll. Use a scale of $\frac{1}{16}'' = 1$ inch. If you won't be teaching sixteenths at your grade level you can just adjust your scale accordingly (e.g. $\frac{1}{8}'' = 2$ inches and so forth). The finished model ruler can be hung along a chalkboard tack strip or mounted permanently to the wall.

Modeling Compounds. A bit of ingenuity is almost always needed in model making. You're almost always trying to let an object represent something that it is not. Many modeling compounds are available in art supply, hobby, and toy shops. These compounds can be molded quite easily, and some will hold rather intricate detail. Most compounds have some slight shrinkage upon use, so allow for it. If molding compounds are too expensive, papier mâché or paper strips can be used for making large objects.

Working with Papier Mâché. Mâché is particularly valuable in making land forms and three-dimensional maps.

Mâché is made by soaking paper pulp (or small pieces of newsprint, about one inch square) in a thick wallpaper wheat paste. The mixture should be allowed to stand, with occasional mixing, until the paper begins to disintegrate. Mâché should not be applied dripping wet; it's best to squeeze out excess paste before application.

Only with very thin models should the mâché be applied to the full depth of the model, since it is actually intended to be only a surfacing material—much like stucco on a house.

To achieve this goal, you'll have to build up a form which is then covered with the mâché. Numerous materials may be used, but various size cardboard boxes and wire window screen material seem to be the favorites. For example, if you want to make a mountain, you could set up 3 different size cardboard boxes, and form the wire screen over them in the desired shape. The paste saturated mâché is then applied to the screen mesh and manipulated into the exact shape desired. If the screen must later be removed, cover it with plastic food wrap before mâché application.

When the shaping process is finished, the mâché should be allowed to air dry slowly. In dry weather, a thin mâché layer (½″) will dry in about two days. Thicker layers, or damp weather, will naturally prolong the process.

The dried model may be painted with standard tempera paints or enamels. If tempera is used, a coat of spray plastic (acrylic) would be a worthwhile protection.

Paper Strips. Some objects do not lend themselves to the papier mâché construction technique. For example, if you want to make a globe, planet, or satellite, mâché is useless. Instead, you can use paste saturated newspaper strips.

Cut the newspaper into strips about 1″ wide and soak them in wallpaper paste immediately before use. The strips will need to soak only a short while since they should not be reduced to pulp before use.

To make a strip globe, inflate a beach ball and cover it completely with petroleum jelly. Then criss-cross the entire surface, except the air

Fig. 9.7—Land form models of lasting value may be constructed from a variety of readily available materials, in addition to mâché. This land form was made from shreaded asbestos (used as furnace insulation) and wheat paste. Finishing touches were added with tempera, poured plaster of Paris (to simulate water) and soap for houses and boats.

valve area, with paste soaked strips to a depth of about ¼ inch (for a 12 to 15 inch diameter ball). After the surface is completely covered to the desired depth, allow the sphere to dry, deflate the ball and cut the globe partially open with a keyhole saw or model knife. Open the globe only enough to allow you to withdraw the deflated ball. The cut may then be repaired with additional paste soaked strips.

The globe should be finished by adding a coat of 2 solution epoxy paint. Or, if you seal it with shellac first, spray paint may be used.

Shadowbox. Model making can be educationally rewarding. But when the model is put in its proper background and perspective, the reward to you and your pupils increases many times. At lower grade levels, this scene usually takes the form of a so-called "shadowbox"— actually any simple box, such as a shoebox, which establishes confining limits to the scene.

As a first stage in scene development, this form might be acceptable, but it leaves much to be desired in the way of realism. The one instance in which the shadowbox is truly legitimate is the exhibition of a room and its contents. Then the square corners of the box are realistic.

The Diorama. Unlike the museum's life-sized habitat group, which presents a reconstructed view of reality, the diorama shows reality in miniature. As such, it is somewhat more versatile than its big brother, since illusions of perspective are quite easy to produce. In the diorama the viewer is given the feeling of "peering in" to a piece of life or nature. The construction of the diorama shell itself is designed to enhance this feeling; and by following a few simple principles and suggestions, most teachers would be able to make a good diorama on the first try.

Diorama construction can be divided into 3 stages:

1. The selection of the theme.
2. Construction of the frame and background.
3. Construction of the scene.

The theme of the diorama will probably be correlated with your course of study, but make certain it's workable, before you decide on it. While almost anything visible can be made into a diorama, some scenes would be so difficult to construct in a life-like manner that the time expended in construction would be far more valuable than the instructional value of the item.

Also, the diorama is designed to present an illusion of reality. Be practical. If reality is at hand, don't waste time making a diorama of it. To the city child, a diorama of farm, silo, farmhouse, and animals might be a valuable learning experience. But to the farm child, it would only be a repeat performance of that which he sees every day.

Some excellent diorama themes which teachers have developed are dinosaurs in the rain forest, a French street scene, a farm, insects in natural habitat (in this instance the diorama would also be a life-size habitat group), and rocket launch pads.

Remember, always select a scene theme which can be developed in perspective, for this is the key to the diorama's strength in presenting the illusion of reality.

Actually, dioramas may be constructed in any proportion which meets your needs. However, according to the nation's leading diorama expert, Dr. Irene F. Cypher, of New York University, a 2:1:1 length to height to depth ratio is a good one for school dioramas, since it preserves the "looking in" feeling, and is small enough to be displayed and stored in limited classroom space.

Of course, in actual practice, the size of the diorama must be variable. The height of objects or models to be used in it to some extent determines the dimensions of the diorama itself. If the objects are relatively small, a suggested size might be 12″ high, by 24″ long, by 12″ deep at the center back.

Here are the steps in constructing a diorama:

1. Obtain 2 pieces of 24″ x 1″ x 1″ and 2 pieces of 12″ x 1″ x 1″ lumber. Make a rectangular frame of them with the shorter pieces placed between the two longer members as shown.

2. Cut a curved back base from a sheet of heavy corrugated board. The base should be designed to make a regular arc to a maximum depth of 12 inches with a 24 inch cord (straight edge). Attach to bottom of frame.

3. Attach a background strip made of flexible chipboard or tagboard to the frame as shown. The background strip may be fastened to the base with masking tape and to the frame (short sides) with staples or brads.

After the background is attached to the frame it should be painted to give an illusion of depth. Since the background is curved, the farthest point in the illusory distance is the center of the background. Accordingly, any objects painted on the background should be smallest toward the center and largest at the two sides.

Actual scene construction will be a credit to your own ingenuity—both in materials to use and in manner of use. Here are some commonly used materials:

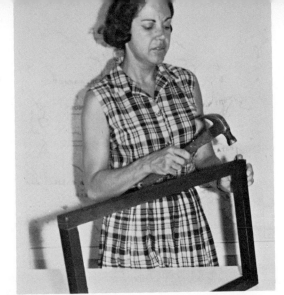

Fig. 9.8A—Making the frame.

Fig. 9.8B—Cutting the base.

Fig. 9.8C—Attaching the background strip.

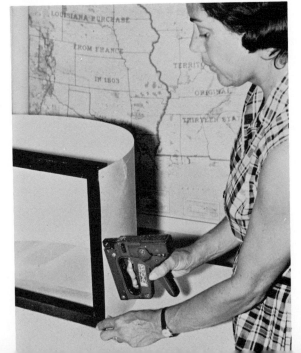

Material	Use
sand	roads, beaches, walks
twigs	trees
sponge	bushes, leaves
wire screen	land form molds
papier mâchè } plaster of Paris plasticene }	cover for land form molds and modeling
dyed sawdust	grass
glass, sheet plastic } cellophane }	water
pipe cleaners	skeletal armatures for figures, shapes, etc.
boxes, construction paper	buildings

Also very useful are the vast variety of model railroad building supplies—which come in assorted sizes suited to various model railroad gauges, but ideal for diorama building. The fact that these materials (trees, bushes, houses, mountains, etc.) come in different sizes is very valuable in creating the illusion of depth, since larger objects in the foreground, and smaller ones to the rear, also create perspective.

Appendix A

PRODUCTS
AND SOURCES

The products listed in this appendix have been referred to in the text matter or may be difficult to locate locally. The list does not include all manufacturers or distributors; rather, it is intended solely as an aid to swift location of materials and supplies discussed in this book.

Mounting and Laminating

Pressure Sensitive Adhesives

Adhesive Products Corporation, 1660 Boone Avenue, Bronx, N.Y. (liquid pressure sensitive adhesive—activates when dry)

Avery Label Co., Monrovia, California (adhesive dots on carrier paper)

Delkote, Inc., Box 1335, Wilmington 99, Delaware (solid, putty-like adhesive)

Kleen-Stik Products, Inc., Chicago, Illinois 60631 (2 sided pure adhesive strip in tape form on carrier tape)

Permacel Adhesives, U.S. Hy 1, New Brunswick, N.J. (psa tapes)

Sears Roebuck & Co., Philadelphia, Pa. 19132, or locally (contact bond cement)

Stick-Tak, 1299 Boyleston St., Boston 15, Mass. (wax type adhesive coated plastic discs)

3 M Company, Adhesive Products Division, St. Paul, Minn. (psa spray, double face tape, ultra-violet passing tape, etc.)

Dry Mounting (heat activated) Supplies and Equipment

Adhesive Products Corp., 1660 Boone Avenue, Bronx, N.Y. (brush-on liquid, heat sensitive when dry)

Eastman Kodak Co., Rochester 4, N.Y. (dry mount tissue)

L. Kaltman & Sons, South Orange, N.J. 07079 (all supplies and equipment)

John G. Marshall Mfg. Co., Inc., 167 9th St., Brooklyn, N.Y. (dry mounting aerosol spray)

Seal, Inc., Shelton, Conn., (all types of dry mounting supplies and equipment)

Laminating Supplies and Equipment

Apeco, 55 East 34th Street, N.Y., N.Y. (equipment and supplies)

Carr Plastics Corporation, Cleveland 15, Ohio (clear plastic laminating sheets, plain and adhesive coated)

General Binding Corporation, 1101 Skokie Blvd., Northbrook, Ill. 60062 (plastic laminating supplies and equipment)

Valiant Industries, 172 Walker Lane, Englewood, N.J. (equipment and supplies)

Other Adhesives

Arthur Brown & Bro., 2 West 46th St., N.Y., N.Y. 10036 (all types of artists' adhesives)

Carter's Ink Co., Cambridge 42, Mass., (epoxy, white plastic, vinyl, polystyrene, household and other adhesives)

Delkote, Incorporated, Box 1335, Wilmington 99, Delaware (white plastic glue)

General Electric Co., Waterford, N.Y. (silicone rubber flexible adhesive)

Montgomery Ward, Albany 1, N.Y., or your area (all types of standard adhesives)

Sears Roebuck & Co., Philadelphia, Pa. 19132, or your area (all types of standard adhesives)

Tri-Tix, Inc., Port Washington, Wisconsin (water base rubber glue)

Flat Graphic Protection Materials

Krylon, Inc., Norristown, Pa. (clear plastic spray)

Arthur Brown & Bro., Inc., 2 W. 46th St., N.Y., N.Y. 10036 (clear plastic sprays, lacquer sprays, clear sheet plastics)

Celanese Corporation of America, 744 Broad Street, Newark, N.J. 07102 (sheet plastic film)

Plasti-Cote Corp., Cleveland 15, Ohio (clear plastic spray)

Seal, Inc., Shelton, Conn. (clear plastic film and application equipment)

Plastic Casting and Embedment

Glass Plastics Corp., 1261 W. Elizabeth Avenue, Linden, N.J. (all casting materials and supplies)

Castolite Co., Woodstock, Illinois (all casting materials and supplies)

local hobby or craft shops

Slide Equipment and Supplies

Lantern Type

Charles Beseler Co., 219 S. 18th St., East Orange, N.J. (inks and coloring materials)

Celanese Corporation of America, 744 Broad Street, Newark, N.J. 07102 (Lumarith® plastic slide material)

Eastman Kodak Co., Rochester 4, N.Y. (photographic lantern slide material)

Keystone View Co., Meadville, Pa. 16335 (all types of supplies and equipment for handmade slides)

Polaroid Corporation, Cambridge, Mass., (Polaroid® lantern slide materials)

Radio Mat Co., 222 Oakridge Rd., Daytona Beach, Fla. (slide carbons)

2 x 2 and Other Photographic Slide Materials

Ansco Corporation, Binghamton, N.Y. (photo film)

Eastman Kodak Co., Rochester 4, N.Y. (photo film)

Spiratone, Inc., 369 Seventh Avenue, N.Y., N.Y. 10001 (slide mounts, trays, film, etc.)

Overhead Projection

Projectors and Attachments

American Optical Co., Instrument Division, Buffalo, N.Y. 14215
Buhl Optical Co., 1009 Beech Avenue, Pittsburgh, Pa. 15233
Charles Beseler Co., 219 So. 18th St., East Orange, N.J.
GAF, 140 W. 51st St., N.Y., N.Y. 10020
Graflex, Inc., Rochester, N.Y. 14603
H. Wilson Co., 546 W. 119th St., Chicago, Ill. 60628
3 M Co., Visual Products, St. Paul, Minn.
Tecnifax Corporation, 195 Appleton St., Holyoke, Mass.
Visual Impact Materials, Inc., 812 E. Apache, Tempe, Arizona 85281 (CIP Overslide® projector—OHP and filmstrip combined)

Transparency Making Supplies and Equipment

American Optical Co., Instrument Division, Buffalo 15, N.Y. (polarization materials)
Charles Beseler Co., 219 So. 18th St., East Orange, N.J. (all types of thermal and diazo supplies and equipment; acetate, mounts, coloring materials, etc.)
Eastman Kodak Co., Rochester 4, N.Y. (all materials for photographic transparencies; also for Ektalith® and Verifax® transparency materials)
GAF, Binghamton, N.Y. 13902 (photocopy and diazo transparency materials and mounts)
Tecnifax Corporation, 195 Appleton, Holyoke, Mass. (all types of handmade and diazo transparency supplies and equipment, polarization kits)
Technical Animations, Inc., 11 Sintsink Drive East, Port Washington, N.Y. (polarization supplies)
3 M Company, Visual Products, St. Paul, Minn. (all types of thermal transparency materials, mounts, pre-printed masters, coloring pens and pencils, etc.)
Valiant Industries, 172 Walker Lane, Englewood, N.J. (thermal and handmade transparency supplies)
Viewlex, Inc., Holbrook, Long Island, N.Y. (thermal transparency making equipment and supplies)

Chart Making Materials

Pre-Printed Lettering, Tapes, Patterns, and Dry Color

ACS Tapes., Inc., 217 California St., Newton 58, Mass. (pre-printed tapes and dry transfer symbols and alphabets)
Arthur Brown & Bro, Inc., 2 West 46th Street, N.Y., N.Y. 10036 (all types of dry transfer and lettering tape materials; Instantype®)
Chart-Pak Inc., River Road, Leeds, Mass. 01053 (plastic base and dry transfer lettering, color, and pattern materials)
Color Stik, 219 So. 18th Street, East Orange, N.J. (translucent color dry transfer letters)
Graphic Associates, 345 Boulevard, Hasbrouck Heights, N.J. (pre-printed letters and symbols on plastic base)

Graphic Products Corp., Rolling Meadows, Illinois 60008 (pre-printed materials on pressure sensitive acetate or polyethelene base)

Paratone Inc., 512 W. Burlington, La Grange, Illinois (pre-printed letters and symbols on plastic base; also patterns)

Russell Industries, Inc., 96 Station Plaza, Lynbrook, N.Y. 11563 (dry transfer materials)

Lettering Pens, Inks, Stencils, and Devices

Arthur Brown & Bro., Inc., 2 W. 46th St., N.Y., N.Y. 10036 (all types)

Beckley-Cardy Co., 1900 N. Narragansett Avenue, Chicago, Illinois 60639 (all types)

Esterbrook Pen Co., Delaware Avenue, Camden, N.J. (drawing pens and flow type markers)

Embossograf Corporation of America, 38 W. 21st St., N.Y., N.Y. (embossed lettering supplies and equipment)

C. Howard Hunt Pen Co., 7th & State Sts., Camden, N.J. (Speedball® lettering pens and inks)

Keuffel & Esser, Hoboken, N.J. (Leroy® template type lettering device)

Letterguide, Box 99, State House Station, Lincoln, Nebraska (template type lettering device)

Pentel Pen Co., 333 N. Michigan Avenue, Chicago, Illinois 60601 (flow pens and markers)

Sanford Ink, Co., Bellwood, Illinois (acetate pens, inks, markers)

Speedry Products, Richmond Hill 18, N.Y. (flow pens, markers, inks)

Stenso Lettering Co., Baltimore 18, Maryland (die cut pressboard stencils)

Valiant Industries, 172 Walker Lane, Englewood, N.J. (markers, pens, acetate inks)

Wood-Regan Instrument Company, Nutley, N.J. (Wrico® system stencils, pens, supplies, and other lettering devices)

Pre-Cut or Formed Letters

Art Brown & Bro., Inc., 2 W. 46th St., N.Y., N.Y. 10036

Mittens Display Letters, 345 5th Street, Redlands, California

Mutual Aids, 1946 Hillhurst, Los Angeles, California

Redi-Cut Letter Co., 185 N. Prairie, Hawthorne, California

Display Boards and Materials

Arthur Brown & Bro., Inc. 2 W. 46th Street, N.Y., N.Y. 10036 (flock, bulletin boards, flannel boards, etc.)

Beckley-Cardy Co., 1900 N. Narragansett, Chicago, Ill. 60639 (all types of display boards)

Charles Mayer Studios, Inc., 776 Commins St., Akron, Ohio 44307 (Velcro® type boards and accessories)

Celotex Corporation, 120 So. LaSalle St., Chicago, Illinois 60603 (wood fiber boards)

Instructo Products Co., 1635 N. 55th St., Philadelphia, Pa. 19131 (flannelboards, magnetboards, devices and materials)

Jacronda Mfg. Co., 5449 Hunter Street, Philadelphia, Pa. (flannelboards and supplies)

The Judy Co., 310 N. 2d Street., Minneapolis 1, Minn. (flannelboards and supplies)

Masonite Corporation, 111 W. Washington St., Chicago, Illinois 60602 (Pegboard® and hardware)

Ohio Flock Cote Co., 5713 Euclid Avenue, Cleveland 3, Ohio (flannelboards, Velcro® boards, and supplies)

U.S. Plywood Corporation, 55 W. 44th St., N.Y., N.Y. 10036 (armored plywood for magnet board construction)

Maggie Magnetic Co., 39 W. 32d Street, N.Y., N.Y. 10001 (magnetic boards and supplies)

Edmund Scientific Co., Barrington, N.J. (alnico, ceramic, and plastic magnets)

Recording Equipment and Supplies

Allied Radio Corporation, 100 N. Western Avenue, Chicago, Illinois 60680 (all types of parts, patch cords, loudspeakers, equipment and supplies)

Lafayette Radio Corporation, 111 Jericho Turnpike, Syosset, L.I., N.Y. 11791 (all types of parts, patch cords, loudspeakers, equipment and supplies)

Switchcraft, Inc., 5555 N. Elston Avenue, Chicago, Illinois 60630 (multiple jack boxes, headphones, and other electronic parts)

Bell and Howell, 7100 McCormick Rd., Chicago, Illinois 60645 (Language Master® specialized tape recorder and supplies)

Cousino, Inc., 2107 Ashland Avenue, Toledo 2, Ohio (cartridge and repeater tape recorders)

Appendix B

TOPIC LOCATOR

INDEX

204

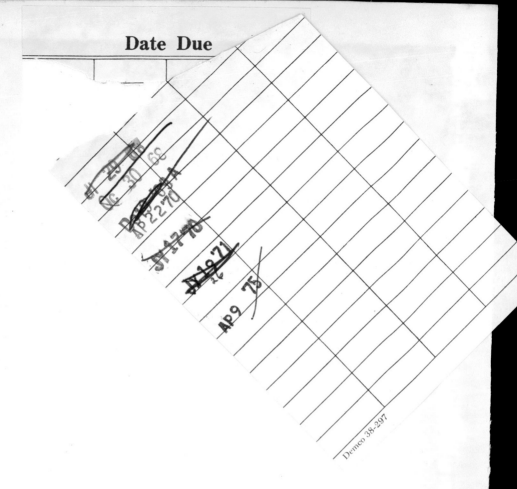